T0167994

The Pet Detective Series

ARE DOGS THE
RIGHT PET FOR YOU?

Can *You* Find out the Facts?

First published 2016

Copyright © Emma Milne 2016

All rights reserved. No part of this publication may be reproduced, stored in a retrieval system, or transmitted, in any form or by any means, electronic, mechanical, photocopying, recording or otherwise, without prior permission of the copyright holder.

Published by

5M Publishing Ltd,
Benchmark House, 8 Smithy Wood Drive, Sheffield, S35 1QN, UK

Tel: +44 (0) 1234 81 81 80
www.5mpublishing.com

A Catalogue record for this book is available from the British Library

ISBN 978-1-910455-71-5

Book layout by Mark Paterson
Printed by CPI, UK

Photos and illustrations by Emma Milne unless otherwise credited

The Pet Detective Series

ARE DOGS THE RIGHT PET FOR YOU?

Can You Find out the Facts?

By

Emma Milne

BVSc MRCVS

For Julie.

THE most dedicated dog owner
in the WHOLE WORLD!

Contents

Acknowledgements

This book would not have been possible without the fantastic support, photos and help from lots of people. Thank you to the wonderful Animal Welfare Foundation, the Blue Cross and the Association of Pet Behaviour Counsellors. Having endorsement from such respected organisations is a great privilege. Huge gratitude also goes to Karen Wild and Ryan Neile for their help on the complex subject of dog behaviour. Massive thanks to Marie Robertson, Julie Irons, Janet Bridson, Susannah Coleman, Su O'Neill, David Gould, Andrew White, Hill's Pet Nutrition, Bayer Animal Health and the PDSA for the use of their great photos. Thank you to Emily Coultish for bringing my cartoon ideas to life and for putting up with my pedantry about details! I salute you all!

Chapter 1

Humans and animals have shared this lovely little planet of ours for thousands of years. Over that time we've used and needed animals in all sorts of different ways. First of all we needed their bodies and we used to use all the bits we could. We ate their meat and some of the other bits too, like kidneys and livers and hearts. We got rich nutrients out of their bones in the bit called the marrow. We used their stomachs to carry water in or to cook other bits in. Animal fat was used to make oils and candles and fuel lamps and torches. Bones and horns could be made into tools and cups and we used their skins and fur to keep us warm and dry. Even things like a bison's tail could be made into anything from a fly swat to an ornament.

"Hey! I'm still using that!"

These days we still eat plenty of animals but we've found substitutes for some of the other bits. Over those thousands of years we started to realise that animals could be useful for other things. Cats were very good at catching mice and rats and other pests that ate our crops, so having cats around started to look like a good thing. They could do jobs for us that we found hard. Wild dogs started creeping closer to human camps to get some warmth from our fires and steal scraps of our food. But in return humans got some protection, thanks to dogs' natural guarding instincts, and we learned that if we joined them in hunting, we made a pretty good team. Horses, donkeys and camels could be tamed and could carry big loads and cover distances that man couldn't even attempt. These animals are still used all over the world today.

As more time has gone by we've stopped needing animals so much to do things for us. We have cars and tractors, we have mouse traps and food containers that can't be chewed through, we have houses with alarms and strong doors and big locks and we have farmed animals to eat, so we no longer need to hunt. But the simple truth is that we found out that animals are wonderful creatures, and in the time we were getting to know each other, humans started to fall in love with just having animals around.

A dog putting his head on your lap to have his ears stroked gets some lovely affection, but the human who's feeling those velvety ears and looking into those lovely brown eyes gets a lot back too. The cat stretched out on a warm rug by the fire has definitely 'landed on its feet', but the doting owner smiling in the doorway just watching the cat's tummy rise and fall with its breathing feels calm and happy without even realising it. Pets make us happy. They make us feel calm and loved and wanted. Pets don't judge us or hold a grudge for days like your best friend did when you spoke to the new girl at school. They are always there and they stick with you through thick and thin. In fact, sometimes they seem a lot nicer to be around than some humans!

The Serious Bit

The last point is the bit that is so important to remember: humans don't always do the right thing for their pets. Pets don't get to decide who buys them or how they are cared for. They have to live wherever you put them and they can only have the food you give them, because they can't get to food themselves. When they go to sleep, how comfortable their bed is will be totally up to you. What you have to realise is that if you want a pet, those animals are *completely* dependent on you and your family to keep them happy, healthy and safe.

It sounds like an easy thing, doesn't it? Buy a cage, or a cat bed or a dog's squeaky toy, go to the pet shop and buy a bag of food and your pet will have everything it needs. WRONG! Thousands if not millions of pets have been kept this way, and of course with food and water most animals can survive for years, but that is just not enough. A great life isn't about coping or managing or *surviving*. It's about being HAPPY! If you were locked in your bedroom with no toys or books or friends or even your pesky sister, you'd *manage*. As long as your mum gave you bread and stew twice a day and the odd bit of fruit you'd probably live for years. But would you be happy? It doesn't sound likely, does it? You'd be bored out of your mind, lonely, miserable and longing for someone to play with, even if it was just that nose-picking sister or brother you usually avoid like a fresh dog poo and make cry in front of your friends.

Having a pet, any pet, is a serious business. It's a bit like getting married or having a tattoo: you definitely shouldn't rush into it! You need to think carefully about lots of things. What sort of house or flat do you live in? How big is your garden if you have one? What other animals, if any, have you already got? How much money do your parents earn? Because I can tell you there is no such thing a cheap pet. How much spare time do you *actually* have? Are you an active family or a lazy one? All these questions have to be asked and they have to be answered very *honestly*. And of course you need to ask yourself what sort of animal do you want?

I've been a bit sneaky there because actually you should *never* ask yourself what sort of animal you want. You should think about what sort of animal you can look after properly. There's a very famous song from a long time ago called 'You Can't Always Get What You Want' and I'm sure your mum or dad will have said it to you hundreds of times. You probably rolled your eyes, walked off in a huff, slammed a door and shouted, 'THAT'S NOT FAIR!!!' But I hate to say that your mum and dad are right, and it's especially true when it comes to keeping pets. Lots of animals get abandoned or given away because people don't ask themselves the right questions, don't find out the facts and then, most importantly, don't answer the questions honestly.

Let's be honest: you lot are masters at pestering. For as long as children, parents and pets have been around, children have pestered, parents have caved in and pets have been bought on an impulse! This means without thinking and without knowing what the animal actually needs to be happy, which usually means a very miserable pet.

But we're about to change all that, aren't we? Because now I've got the dream team on my side. You chose to find out the facts about these animals so you *could* make the right choice. And I am very proud of you for that and I am very happy. So thank you.

The EVEN MORE serious bit!

So, you are thinking it would be nice to have a pet. You're certain you are going to love it, care for it, keep it happy and, of course, NEVER get bored with looking after it and expect your mum and dad to do it. But what you need to know is that not only is that the right thing to do, but it is also now the law. Sounds serious, doesn't it, but as I said, it's a serious business. In the United Kingdom in 2006 a new law was made called the Animal Welfare Act. This law says that anyone over the age of sixteen looking after an animal has a 'duty of care' to provide for all the needs of the animal. Now, laws are always written by people who use ridiculously long words and sentences that no-one else really understands, but this law is very important to understand. A duty of care means it is the owner's responsibility to care for the animal properly, and the law means that if the owner doesn't, they could get their pet taken away and even, in rare cases, end up going to prison!

Aha, you may think, I am not sixteen so I'm fine, and you'd be right, but the duty of care then falls to your mum or dad or whoever looks after you and the pet.

THE JOYS OF LIVING WITH ANIMALS.

So if you would like a dog, not only do you need to know all about them, you need to make sure the adults in the house do too. And you need to make sure they know about the law, because they might not know what they are letting themselves in for!

If you don't live in the UK you need to find out what laws there are in your country about looking after animals. But remember, even if your country doesn't have any laws like this, making sure your animals are healthy *and* happy is still simply the right thing to do.

Well, that's quite enough of all the boring serious stuff. Let's learn some things about animals! The easiest way to find out about animals is to know about the five welfare needs. These apply to all pets, and in fact all animals, so they are good things to squeeze into that brilliant brain of yours so you can always remember them whenever you think about animals.

The Need for Fresh Water and the Right Food

This is a very obvious thing to say, but you'd be surprised how many animals get given the wrong food. In fact, there was once a queen a very long time ago who wanted a zebra. I said wanted, didn't I? She definitely didn't ask herself the right questions or find out the facts, because when someone caught her one from the wild, she fed it steaks and tobacco!

Animals have evolved over a very long time to eat certain things, and if they are fed the wrong foods they can get very ill, very fat, or miss vitamins and minerals they might need more than other animals. The right food in the right amounts is essential.

The Need to Be With or Without Other Animals

Some animals live in groups and love to have company. Some animals are not very sociable at all, like me in the mornings! It's very important to know which your pet prefers. If you get it wrong, you could have serious fighting and injuries or just a very lonely and miserable pet.

The Need for the Right Environment

This is a fancy way of saying where the animal lives. It could be a hutch, a cage, a house, bedding, shelter, a stable or lots of other things, depending on the pet. It's very important that their homes are big enough, are clean, are safe and secure and the animals have freedom to move around.

The Need To Behave Naturally

Knowing what animals like to do is really important. As we said before, lots of animals will survive on food and water, but happiness, or 'mental wellbeing', is just as important as being healthy or having 'physical wellbeing'. You've probably never thought about your own behavioural needs but imagine how you would feel if you were never allowed to go to the park or play or run or see your friends. You would soon be quite unhappy. Often you find that happy pets stay healthier, just like us.

The Need to Be Protected from Pain, Injury and Disease

Animals can get ill just like us and it will be up to you and your family to keep your pet healthy as well as happy. Just like you have vaccinations, they are very important for some animals to stop them getting ill and even dying. Animals, just like lots of children, also get worms, lice, mites and other parasites. You will need to find out how to treat or prevent these and look out for signs of them.

You need to check your animals over at least once a day to make sure there are no signs of problems and take them to a vet as soon as you think something is wrong. Vet costs are not cheap. You might also have a pet you can get health insurance for, which is always a good idea.

So now you know the basic needs of all animals, it's time to concentrate on dogs!

Dogs may have been around us humans in one shape or another for a long time, but they still have some wild instincts and needs. The best way to learn what will keep your pet dogs happy and healthy is to find out what dogs in the wild are like. How do they live? What do they eat? Do they like to have others around and what makes them scared? In other words, what keeps them HAPPY? Shall we begin?

Dogs — guardians, friends and part of the family.

Chapter 2

DOGS IN THE WILD.

Looking at how our pets started out and how they and their wild relatives live *without* human beings getting in the way is the best way to understand how to keep them happy when we do interfere!

Dogs are part of a big group called canids. As well as pet and wild dogs, this group has all the other doggy-type animals in it like wolves, jackals, foxes and the cartoon Roadrunner's famous enemy the coyote. Although canids can be quite different sizes, there are lots of things they have in common. They tend to have ears that stand up straight, long muzzles, long legs and bushy tails.

They usually like to live in groups called packs, and like us humans, they are social creatures.

Canids are social creatures and live in groups.

Canids have erect ears, long legs and muzzles and usually a nice, big bushy tail!

Canids, like our pet dogs today, communicate with body language and sounds. They have lots of ways of expressing a whole range of emotions. They can bare their teeth, raise their hackles and growl to say, 'BEWARE!' They might lick each others' faces when they meet up and many wag their tails when they are happy and relaxed. Lots of canids also bark, whine, growl and howl in different situations.

CANID FACT:

When a wolf howls, it can sometimes be heard over an area of 130km². That's about the size of the whole city of San Francisco!

Howling can be heard from miles around.

© iStock

One of the best ways to understand animals and virtually everything about them is to find out about what they like to eat and what, if anything, eats them. Every animal on the planet has to eat to survive, so food and water are the most important things to them. Animals in the wild never really know when their next meal might be, and getting food can be really hard for them. Let's face it, they can't exactly order a takeaway when they're tired after a hard day!

Over the millions of years that life has existed on our beautiful planet, animals and plants have evolved together in an amazing balance of nature, all based on food chains. Food chains are the way we look at which animals eat what. For example, a simple food chain for a canid like a fox might be:

Fox food chain.

In this food chain the rabbit is what we call the prey, because it is eaten by the fox. The fox is the predator because it eats the rabbit. Predators and prey have usually evolved very differently because of the ways they need to get food. If you're a rabbit, food might be easy to find because grass is everywhere, but you always have to be on the lookout for what might be about to eat you! The rabbit, like lots of prey animals, has eyes on the side of his head so that he can see all around him and above him all at the same time. He needs to be very alert and also very quick to escape if a predator comes along.

DOGS IN THE WILD.

On the other hand, the fox, like all canids, needs to be clever, fit and fast. He needs to outsmart the rabbit and creep up on him without being heard or seen. He also needs to have great senses to find the rabbit in the first place. Canids have an excellent sense of smell and can sniff out their prey from long distances or even under deep snow, depending on where they live. For tackling big animals like antelope and wildebeest, canids have to work together, hunt in groups and communicate well to launch a successful attack. They often chase big prey until the animals are totally tired out, so they need to be really fit and have lots of stamina for running for a very long time.

Most predators have eyes right on the front of their face, like humans, dogs and cats. This means they can't see behind them like rabbits can, but they can judge distance and depth really well for catching fast moving things. Don't forget though that even though teachers are humans and have forward-facing eyes, they can still see what you are doing behind them without moving their heads!

Of course, when you think about it, lots of animals are predators and prey at the same time. Humans are one of the most successful predators on the planet but there are still plenty of things that can make a meal of us given the chance.

Canids have to work together to tackle large prey.

© iStock

Human in food chain.

Dogs' wild relatives are just the same. In Africa and places where there are big predators like lions, smaller canids such as the African wild dog have to be very careful not to get badly injured or killed by other predators that might want to steal their food. And remember, no animal *wants* to get eaten, so prey animals usually have things to defend themselves, like horns, antlers and powerful legs and hooves. These can all badly wound the hunting canids, so they have to be super careful to stay out of the way until the time is right.

Man's Best Friend

Dog lovers all over the world think of their dogs as man's best friend, but where did they come from? Modern day dogs are all sorts of shapes and sizes, but they all started out roughly the same. We think that dogs evolved from types of wolves in Europe and Asia, probably about 40,000 years ago!

DOG FACT:

In a cave in France explorers have found the footprints of a young child of around ten years of age and a large dog or wolf. The footprints show the dog and the child are walking next to each other and are about 26,000 years old!

DOG FACT:

Dogs are one of the only animals on the planet that can understand what it means when a human points at something. It seems hard to believe that any animals could *not* understand it, doesn't it? It seems so obvious to us. You can test it out for yourself. Next time you're at a friend's house and they have a cat, point at something near the cat.

As we said, canids like wolves and dogs are social creatures and live and hunt in groups. Judging by the cave in France, it seems that dogs and humans made a good team from pretty early on. Dogs got the benefit of our warm fires and scraps of leftover food and humans got the benefit of help with sniffing out food, super-fit hunting buddies and the way dogs naturally guard their territory and look after their family and friends.

Cats aren't stupid but the cat will probably totally ignore you, stare at you like you are mad or sniff your finger and walk off. Do the same thing to a friend's dog and the dog will look at where you're pointing and go and see what it is. Brilliant!

Chapter 2

DOGS IN THE WILD.

So if dogs started out like wolves and were the same as most of the other canids, how did they get to be so different? All the different breeds of dog we have these days only came about pretty recently in the last few hundred years. This might seem like a long time to us, but compared to how long humans and dogs have been friends, it's not very long at all.

To start with, humans probably started to pick dogs that seemed very good at one thing or another and bred from them, for instance, dogs that were good at guarding and dogs that were better at herding or hunting. As time goes by you might end up with smaller hunting dogs that were good at going down rabbit holes and big ones that were better at hunting big animals like deer. This way you would end up with different types of dogs.

© iStock

Over the years, as we said in the last chapter, humans started to realise that just having dogs around is really lovely and they make good companions. They are loyal and loving and they don't judge us like humans do. They are playful and fun and they make us smile. Also in lots of countries now we don't *need* dogs to hunt or guard for us, so they have become pets. But humans love to tinker with things and so they have kept on breeding dogs and making new breeds. So now we have all sorts of shapes and sizes and hundreds of different breeds of dog instead of just a few different types. We'll talk about this a bit more later on when we look at dogs' needs and also when we talk about their health.

For now, though, you know pretty much everything there is to know about wild canids, dogs' relatives, and where modern dogs came from, so we'd better get down to the tricky business of keeping dogs as happy, healthy pets.

© Suzanne O'Neill

Did someone say dinner time? Wait for me!

FRESH WATER AND THE RIGHT FOOD.

We've already said that a great life is what we should try to give all our pets, and the best start to that is to get the basic survival stuff exactly right from the very start. The top three things needed for life are air, water and food. Animals, including humans, can't live without these things, and when it comes to food, getting the right diet and feeding the right *amounts* of food will get your dog off to a brilliant start for a healthy and happy life.

Let's tackle the easy part first. Water. Water is absolutely essential for every living thing on Earth. For animals like humans and dogs, after the need for air, water is the most important thing. If animals can't get to enough water they can get very ill and die really quickly. Water is the only thing your dog needs to have to drink. Depending on the food you give them, they might also get some water in their food, say for instance in tinned food, but it's essential they have access to plenty of fresh water all the time as well. Some people, when they are trying to house-train puppies, take their water away at night to try to stop them having a wee in the house. You must never do this. Young animals need food and water much more often than older animals. It can be dangerous and cruel to deprive an animal of water, so make sure they have it all the time.

Just like us, they will need to drink more during warm weather compared to cold weather and also if they've been very active, running around and playing.

Some dogs are very messy drinkers and dribble and splash water all over the place after they've finished drinking. You might want to consider this when you're thinking about where to put their bowl, because you'll probably want it to be somewhere that is easy to dry and keep clean.

FRESH WATER AND THE RIGHT FOOD.

So, first we need air, then water and then of course we need food. Bodies are amazingly clever and make any computer or machine that humans have built look like the most rubbish toy imaginable. Like all machines, bodies need energy to make them work. Because our bodies are so spectacularly clever, they can also fix themselves and replace their own parts. Instead of plastic and metal bits or replacement batteries, they need vitamins and minerals, fibre, proteins, fats and carbohydrates. All animals get these from their food, and over the millions of years that animals have been on the planet, they have evolved different ways to get all the things they need from their foods. As we said, wild dogs hunt in groups for their fresh meat but also scavenge a wide variety of food and scraps.

DOG FACT:

Dogs are in the family of animals called Carnivora, which means meat eaters, but from a diet point of view modern dogs are actually omnivores like bears and humans. This means they eat plants as well as meat. They evolved next to us by eating our scraps and are now very good at eating foods besides meat like grain and vegetables. In this way they are very different to their wolfy ancestors.

So what do we feed pet dogs? Are you going to have to get a load of your friends' dogs together with yours and go out hunting and killing animals together? NO! Of course not! Phew.

The great thing is that we live in a time where we know absolutely *loads* about what animals need to eat and what they need in order to grow perfectly, live healthily and then grow old well too. All the work has been done for us and there are dozens of brands of dog food we can choose from. Now the only thing we have to do is pick which one to feed! If you do get a dog or puppy, have a chat with your vet right at the start or, even better, *before* you get your dog to find out what food they recommend and why. Most dog foods will provide everything your dog needs, but some are better than others. Most vets recommend what we call 'super premium' foods. This means they don't just meet your animal's basic needs: they have good quality ingredients, they are very strictly controlled so they are always balanced and they have the little extras in them for tip top health.

Growth

Growing up is hard work and it takes lots more food and nutrients than being an adult does. You may have heard your mum or dad say they wish they could eat as much as they used to. When I was a little girl I used to eat about eight Weetabix a day as well as all my normal food. My bones and muscles were growing, my brain was developing and I was always running, skipping, jumping, doing cartwheels and climbing trees. Nowadays I eat about half what I used to because I'm not growing anymore, I don't have the energy to run about and last time I tried a cartwheel I pulled a muscle!

Growing animals (and kids) need more calories (or energy), more protein and more of certain minerals than adults. They also need things called fatty acids to help their eyes and brains develop as best as they can.

It's really important to feed puppy food to puppies. It sounds obvious, doesn't it, but lots of people don't. You might find your puppy would survive on adult food, but if you want it to grow properly and be the healthiest, brainiest dog it can be, you need to feed it good-quality puppy food. If you have a puppy that is going to be a big dog when it grows up, it should be fed large-breed puppy food. This is because bigger dogs take longer to mature and need to grow a little bit more slowly. If they grow too quickly they can get problems with their joints and bones that can be really horrible and difficult to correct later in life.

This is a good place to talk about dry food and wet food. Just as it sounds, dry food is the dry kibble biscuits you get and wet food is the meaty-looking food you get in tins, pouches or little foil trays. Some wet foods are chunks in gravy and some are more pâté-style tinned foods. Virtually all foods are 'complete' now, which means they provide everything your dog needs, but do check that whatever food you pick is complete. In general it doesn't matter if you feed wet or dry because both should provide everything.

© Hill's Pet Nutrition

You can feed dry food...

© Suzanne O'Neill

...or tinned food or a combination of both.

Chapter 3

FRESH WATER AND THE RIGHT FOOD.

Dry food usually works out a lot cheaper than wet food, it's easier to store and is not so messy, so lots of people just feed dry food these days. Some people like their dogs to have some wet food as well. It doesn't really matter which you do as long as you make sure what you're feeding is good-quality dog food and is balanced and complete.

So, logically, if we feed puppy food to puppies, we should feed adult food to adults and mature dog food to older dogs. These various foods might be called different things and different brands might have different age guides, so just check with your vet about what to feed when.

Just as important as feeding the right food is feeding the right *amount* of food. Lots of animals have really different calorie needs. This is how much energy they need. As we'll see, some dogs are very active, especially when they're young, while some love to chill out more and are a bit lazy, just the same as some humans are very sporty and some definitely aren't! If you feed both these dogs the same amount of food, the very lazy one could quickly start to get way too fat.

Being too fat, or obesity as it is called, is a real problem for animals and humans alike. You don't find fat animals in nature. Some animals will build up stores of fat to keep them warm and give them energy through the winter, but you will never find a truly fat animal in the wild. Being too fat can give lots of animals diseases and the extra weight puts strains on joints and bones and gives the heart too much work to do. You can imagine that a fat predator would never manage to catch any prey so would never get fat in the first place. And a fat prey animal might struggle to get away from a predator and wouldn't live long enough to have fat babies. This really is survival of the fittest!

"Well, this is going to be easy!"

We'll talk more about obesity in Chapter 7, but for now all we need to know is that the right diet and the right amount of food is really important.

Most dog foods have a guide on them to give you an idea of how much your dog will need a day. As dogs are so many different shapes and sizes and types, their food needs vary massively. The guides are usually based on your dog's weight and age but are still just a guide. It's up to you to watch out for if your dog is too thin or fat. Sadly these days so many animals are too fat that people have got used to them looking that way and can't tell the difference any more.

To get it right it's really useful to know about something called body condition score, or BCS. This is a way people like vets judge how fat or thin or just right an animal is. We give a score out of 5, where 1 is dangerously thin, 2 is underweight, 3 is just right, 4 is overweight and 5 is dangerously obese.

© PDSA

© PDSA

© PDSA

Being too fat is no fun for animals and can be very bad for them.

Knowing about BCS is essential for all the best owners.

Body condition score

1
Very thin
• Very little muscle
• Easily seen ribs, backbone and hipbones
• No body fat

2
Underweight
• Clearly seen ribs and backbone
• A little fat over hipbones
• Obviously tucked-in waist

3
Ideal
• Can feel ribs, backbone and hipbones, but not prominent
• Smooth, curved, tucked-in waist
• Base of tail smooth

4
Overweight
• No waist and back broader
• Ribs, backbone and hipbones difficult to feel
• Fat at base of tail

5
Obese
• Bulging pot belly
• Cannot feel ribs, backbone or hipbones
• Thick fatty pads at base of tail

pdsa.org.uk

pd**e**sa
HELP A VET HELP A PET

FRESH WATER AND THE RIGHT FOOD.

Have a chat with your vet or vet nurse to show you on your dog what to look and feel for. If you can stop them getting fat in the first place it's much easier than trying to get the weight back off again!

There's one more really important thing to say about feeding dogs before we move on, and that is to do with human foods. We've already said that dogs evolved alongside humans by eating our scraps and are good at digesting all sorts. BUT it's very important to know that lots of human foods are also very poisonous to dogs. Things like chocolate, sweeteners, onions, garlic and raisins are just a few. You might wonder how dogs managed over all the other years, but lots of the things we cook and eat now weren't around when humans and dogs starting to hang out together and lots of dogs probably died or got poorly without anyone really understanding why until now.

Lots of people also like the idea of feeding bones and raw meat to dogs, because they feel like it's more like what they would eat in the wild like wolves do. The trouble is that dogs aren't used to this sort of food any more, just like humans don't eat lots of raw meat any more. Some dogs might be absolutely fine but some can get broken teeth, very bad sickness and diarrhoea and even get bones stuck in their intestines and get very ill indeed. Raw meat can also have lots of bacteria and other bugs on it. Even if dogs don't get sick when they eat it, they can spread these germs when they have a poo and it can be very dangerous to people and other dogs.

DOG FACT:

Dogs aren't just different to wolves because they can digest plants like us. Wolves are so super active that they need to eat *three* times as much as our pet dogs. This means that trying to feed dogs as if they were wolves can be a disaster in more ways than one!

By far the safest thing to do is stick to dog food and the occasional treats designed for dogs to enjoy. This way you can be sure you won't get it wrong and make your dog poorly. If you're ever unsure, talk to your vet.

Now we know all about what pet dogs need to eat and drink, let's look at what they need next. You'll see as we go along that the next three needs are all closely linked: the right environment, the need to be with or without other animals and the need to express normal behaviour. Shall we get started?

I'm off!

© Suzanne O'Neill

Chapter 4

THE RIGHT ENVIRONMENT.

Dogs are very happy to share YOUR environment

© Marie Robertson

EASY! YOUR PLACE!

Hang on a minute: maybe we should investigate a bit more than that. Now we know what complex creatures dogs are, it's probably not as simple as we imagine.

DOG FACT:

A good way to avoid having your house, shoes and belongings destroyed is to adopt an older dog. Usually it's puppies and very young dogs that are the demolition experts. There are lots of lovely dogs in adoption centres waiting for homes, and that are well past the chewing phase, so why not pop along to your local centre and have a look?

It's probably easiest to look first at all the things dogs need from you when it comes to their environment. Then we can look at all the things dogs might do to their environment, and that you need to be prepared for!

In lots of ways dogs are easy to keep as pets because they don't need a big hutch, cage or run like rabbits, guinea pigs and some other pets. They generally just share your house and garden. But there are things that they will need and more importantly there are things they might do that you or your family might not like, so you need to be prepared for that! You also need to consider the things in your house that could be dangerous for your dogs. Dogs can be very mischievous especially when they are young. They can chew things, steal things from worktops and even open cupboards sometimes. So you'll need to start to see your house from a dog's point of view and make sure things are hidden away. Every vet in the country will have loads of stories about the weird and wonderful things they have had to take out of dogs' tummies: socks, pants, rocks, Kinder eggs, rubber balls, peach stones, corn on the cob, marbles, and the list goes on. Basically if it's smaller than a coffee table, the chances are your dog will be able to destroy it and eat it!

Things Dogs Need

Let's start with the basics – somewhere to sleep and something to eat and drink from. Food and water bowls are pretty easy and there are plenty to choose from. You just need to think about how big your dog might end up, or be prepared to change the bowls as he grows.

Our cheeky cat Brian thought our dog bowls were very cosy!

Chapter 4

THE RIGHT ENVIRONMENT.

As for somewhere to sleep, well... Dogs are social creatures and lots of them like to sit with their friends. Which is you! We always had a rule that our dogs were not allowed on the furniture or in the bedrooms because we didn't want mud and dog hair everywhere, but it's really up to you (or strictly speaking your mum or dad) whether you let them on the furniture or not.

© Susannah Coleman

Lots of dogs are allowed on the furniture, but you need to be consistent.

You need to stick to your decision, though, because your dog won't understand if one day he's welcome on the sofa and the next day he's not. It's also worth bearing in mind that if you take your dog to someone else's house or a pub or restaurant, he will probably think the same rules apply, so choose wisely!

There are hundreds of types of dog beds you can choose from, and even if your dog is allowed on the settee, you should have a bed for him as well, preferably somewhere quiet. Lots of beds are designed for the dog to curl up in, but dogs love to stretch out too, so if you get a curly-up one make sure you have a flat one too so he always has the choice.

Big dogs will need big beds ...

© Susannah Coleman

... little dogs need little beds ...

... and sometimes there will need to be room for two!

© Julie Irons

When you're choosing a bed, think about the type of dog you're getting. If you've opted for an energetic, love-all-weather type dog like a collie, then the bed needs to be very easy to keep clean because your dog won't be! Depending on the weather where you live, virtually all dogs will get dirty from time to time. Even if you have a dog that looks at you as if you are mad if you suggest he goes in the garden or out for a walk when it's raining the mud will find you, believe me! With this in mind you'll need some old towels for drying your dog off and wiping his feet when you get back from muddy walks.

Believe me, the mud will find you!

Talking of walks, your dog will also need a collar and lead and probably a tag with your contact details on it. You need to find out the law where you live. In lots of places it is the law that your dog must wear a collar all the time he's out of the house, with your details on it in case he gets lost. In fact many countries insist on microchipping now too, but we'll talk about that later.

There are plenty of collars and leads to choose from and you can be ultra-fashionable or just practical — that's up to you. What you must never buy are choke chains, electric shock collars or collars designed to spike or pinch your dog's neck. We're going to talk about behaviour a lot in the coming chapters. For now, all you need to know is that using these horrible collars won't stop your dog pulling or misbehaving: they will just hurt him and ruin your friendship.

Stick to a good, strong, comfortable collar and a lead long enough for the size of dog you're getting. Of course you'll need to start off with smaller ones for puppies and change them as they grow. You can also get harnesses to use out on a walk, which take the pressure off your dog's neck. These are fine — just make sure you have the right size. Remember, though, that your dog might still need to have a collar as well if it's the law, and having a tag is always handy in case he runs off or gets lost.

Chapter 4

Space. All dogs need some space no matter what size they are. You don't *have* to have a garden to have a dog, but if you don't, you need to be committed and prepared to take him out every time he might need a wee or a poo. Having a garden makes life easier for you and much nicer for your dog. But remember, having a garden doesn't mean you don't have to take him for a walk.

Having a garden is nice...

© Janet Bridson

...but nothing compares to the great outdoors!

© Susannah Coleman

26

Dogs need space not only to go to the loo and play, but most importantly to *escape* from you! This may sound silly, but dogs need to be able to take themselves away somewhere quiet when they need or want to. You might love your brother or sister but I bet you don't want to be with them *all* the time. Pets need choices too and if your dog wants some peace and quiet, he needs to have somewhere to find it. You might have loads of screechy friends round who think it's OK to maul your dog (it's *not*, but more of that later!), or your brother might be playing a horribly loud video game. Whatever it is, you should respect the freedom of your pets to choose when they want to be alone.

If you live in a one-bedroom flat or have a house that is totally full of people, then you might need to think of a different pet. Of course you can use that brilliant brain and have a family talk and look at ways you might be able to create more room. You never know, your mum and dad might be over the moon to get rid of some of those toys you've been hoarding since the day you were born!

Things your Dog Will Do to your Environment!

Dogs are my favourite pet animals. They are loyal, beautiful, fun and wonderful to have around, BUT they can drive you mad, they can be a real handful and when they are little (and sometimes when they are big) they can be a massive pain in the bum!

You'll see time and again in this book that dogs these days are so different from each other that they're almost like different species. As we said right at the beginning, getting a dog is like getting married. You need to think long and hard about it, you need to be very honest about the sort of person or family you are and you need to pick a dog (or husband or wife!) who makes a great team with you and suits your lifestyle.

Lots of dogs (and husbands and wives!) get given away because of the chaos and havoc they wreak in their owners' lives, and almost every time this happens it is the owner's fault, not the dog's. The fantastic thing about dogs compared to pets like cats is that you can train them. Some are easier to train than others, but in general dogs love to please, and once they know what pleases you they will love to do it over and over again. There are some things about dogs that you can't change, though, no matter how clever they are.

THE RIGHT ENVIRONMENT.

If you are going to welcome one or more dogs into your house and garden, you and your family need to be prepared for mess. Every dog is covered in hair: some have more than others and some shed more than others, but if you have dogs, you'll have hair and dust which will need cleaning up.

As we said, lots of dogs are messy drinkers, some are quite slobbery and some are also messy eaters and like to move their food around the house before they eat it. Some will bury it in odd places like down the settee and in their beds for you to find when it starts to rot. If your mum and dad like the house to look like a show home from a magazine, then a dog is not the ideal pet for you. And don't forget your garden. Dog wee sometimes leaves big bare patches on the lawn and there'll be poo to pick up. Some dogs just love to dig and you'll be surprised how far they can go!

Our dog Pan after being clipped. All this hair could be all over your house!

© Marie Robertson

Your mum or dad may not appreciate this!

© Andrew White

Of course, all this assumes that you are planning to have a dog that lives in your house. Lots of people all over the world choose to keep dogs outside. This is fine too, but there are some things you'll need to consider for your dog's outside environment too.

Firstly, you'll need to make sure you've picked the type of dog that will manage outside wherever you live. Lots of this will depend on the weather and the amount of space you have. If it gets very cold in the winter, you'll need to be absolutely certain that your dog will be warm enough, be out of draughts and winds and always have shelter if it's raining. On the other hand you'll also need to be aware of hot days and make sure your dog can stay cool and get out of the sun and always, no matter what the temperature is, that he has fresh water.

Letting your dog live outside is not an alternative to going for walks and having stimulation. In lots of ways, outside dogs need more interaction and time from you because they are missing out on family life. We're going to talk about the need to be with or without other animals next, but if you are planning to have an outside dog, you should have more than one, because dogs need company.

The last thing to say about outdoor dogs is that they should never be left tied up. This can be dangerous if they get tangled up and it stops them being able to choose what they want to do and where they want to go. If you thought that you could have a dog tied up outside, a nice clean house and just play when you wanted to, then you need to think again.

Ooh, that all got a bit serious again, didn't it? Well, life isn't all fun even though we'd like it to be. BUT, we can make life fun for our pets. We've looked at the basic things dogs need in their environment to get off to a good start, but there are plenty of other things that will make life much better for them. Toys, exercise, fun, games and walks all make life fun for dogs. These are things we call environmental enrichment. Sounds fancy, doesn't it, but it just means making where and how they live better. You might have a big bedroom or house, but if it didn't have books, games, a TV or family and friends in it you would get pretty bored very quickly. It's just the same for our pets. Let's have a look at how we can make life better than basic for dogs with their next two needs.

Chapter 5

If you're shocked about rabbits, guinea pigs and cats, then you'd better get those Pet Detectives books next, but for now we must focus those brilliant brains of yours on dogs.

As we said so many times before, the best way to make sure our pets are happy is to look at their wild relatives and how they evolved and like to live. All the way back in Chapter 2 we said that dogs are canids, like wolves, jackals and wild dogs, and they are social creatures that live and hunt in groups. They like the company of animals the same as them.

© iStock

Dogs and their relatives are social creatures.

© iStock

This is probably the need that humans have messed up the most over all the time we've kept animals as pets. For hundreds of years we've kept rabbits and guinea pigs on their own, rabbits *with* guinea pigs, left dogs alone for hours while we're out and got used to the 'crazy cat ladies' who have dozens of cats in a tiny house. As you may have guessed, ALL THIS IS WRONG!

Although some people don't seem very friendly, we are a social species too, which means it should be easy for us to empathise with dogs. Empathy is when you can imagine how a person or an animal would feel in a similar situation. For example, if you saw a dog that had been starved, you could empathise because you know what it feels like to be hungry. If you saw a cat being chased by a dog, you could empathise with the cat because you know what it feels like to feel frightened. Imagine how you feel when you have to walk past the school bully. Would you rather do it alone or with a group of your friends? Social creatures feel happiest and safest when they are not alone.

Imagine how you would feel if you were never allowed to see your friends, and your family only saw you for a few hours a day. You wouldn't have anyone to tell your funny stories to, you would have no one to play with and you would be extremely bored very quickly. In fact when humans are left completely on their own they actually go totally mad very quickly. Social animals that are left alone, sometimes even only for a little while, also go a bit mad and can have very sad lives. Dogs are just the same.

Human Friends

Now, as we know, dogs and humans have been friends for thousands and thousands of years and lots of dogs these days are very happy to have humans as their family group. But way too many people still think it's OK to leave their dog at home alone for ages while they are out at work or out having fun. It's not!

Dogs need company and stimulation, and some, like puppies and young 'teenager' dogs, need more than others. There's not really a set time that it's OK to leave a dog, but lots of people use four hours as a rough guide. The trouble with giving a rough guide like this is that people like to bend rules, and even ignore them altogether! So lots of people get a dog and go to work and school five days a week, if not more. The dog stays at home alone for four hours in the morning, someone rushes in for lunch, lets the dog out for a wee in the garden, gives him a quick pat on the head, stuffs a sandwich into themselves and rushes back to work for another four hours. That dog has spent seven and a half hours out of eight completely alone. The family then arrive a bit later, it's manic as ever, it's teatime, bath time, homework and bedtime and the dog's alone all night. Even if the family spend all day at the weekends with the dog and all evening in the week, it still means that the dog is alone for well over *half its life!* It doesn't take a genius to realise that this isn't really what the dog wants.

Chapter 5

I'm going to tell you a lot of times in this book that it is not OK to deprive an animal of one of its needs because it is inconvenient for you and your family. Later on, you'll be doing your proper trial month and will really start to see if you have the time and energy to properly give a dog a great life, but now is the time to start seriously thinking about it. If you know that your mum and dad both work and the house is empty most of the time, then a dog is definitely not the right pet for you.

You might be thinking that you know lots of friends who have a dog that spends lots of time on its own and your friend thinks is totally happy. The trouble is that the dog is probably just putting up with it and hasn't quite gone bonkers yet, but that definitely doesn't mean he's happy. Maybe you can lend those friends this book after you've finished with it?

While we are talking about dogs not being left alone too long, we also need to remember that *all* dogs will have to be left alone occasionally. Some dogs never get used to being alone and it can cause lots of upset for the dogs and the humans because dogs that get scared on their own can wreck houses because they are so worried. It's a brilliant idea right from the start to get your dog used to periods of quiet, alone time because it will help all of you in the long run.

Getting your dog used to being alone
– top tips from the Blue Cross

🐾 **Don't give your dog attention all the time.** When you first get a dog, you will be overwhelmingly happy and want to play with him, train him, talk to him, pat him and sometimes even just stare at him all the time (even more than your phone, would you believe!?). Now your dog will get used to everything being about him and think that having constant attention is what life with you is all about. Being the centre of attention and being constantly excited is exhausting for any dog. You can easily imagine as well that when he gets left alone it will seem really different to what he's got used to. He needs to be used to being ignored sometimes so he can learn to relax.

🐾 **Make time alone part of normal life.** Imagine you've had a really long day at school. Your brain hurts and it's full of maths and, even worse, history! You get home from school and your mum gushes all over you, she wants to know who you played with, what lessons you had, if you had any problems, what you learnt, where your PE kit is, and the list goes on. All you really want to do is sit with your mouth slightly open staring at the TV in peace and tranquillity.

When you get a dog, you might notice that when you move round the house your dog wants to follow you everywhere you go. At first you might find this cute but after a while it could get annoying and it makes your dog get used to being with you all the time. Get a stair gate like babies have, and when you leave a room, leave your dog behind, just for a few minutes to start with. Don't make a big fuss when you leave the room or when you come back. This just makes him think that you leaving and going is something to get excited or upset about. You have to act calm and normal as if it is the most normal thing in the world for you to disappear from time to time. Using a stair gate is great because he can still smell, hear and see you to start with.

You should also do this when you leave the house. No fuss! Dogs will start to notice the signs of you going ages before you go. They soon learn that getting bags and coats and shoes out is a sure sign that the humans are about to vanish. If he's used to little bits of time alone every day, he'll be super-cool about you being properly gone.

🐾 **Give him a sign it's quiet or alone time.** We just said your dog will be expert at spotting when you're about to leave, so you can use this to help him get used to it. You can have a sign for quiet time when you are still in the house. Lay a towel or blanket out or put a certain ornament somewhere before you leave the room. It might sound strange, but as you gradually build up time away from your dog, having a sign like this can help him know what's about to happen so he feels in control and can relax. You know that when your mum grabs her keys and screams, 'NURSERY!' before she frantically runs from the house, it means she'll be back soon and is just going to get your pesky sister, but it's taken a long time for you to learn that and feel relaxed about it. Dogs have no idea what we mean if we fuss over them saying, 'I'll be

THE NEED TO BE WITH OR WITHOUT OTHER ANIMALS.

back soon, it's OK, it's OK, it's OK.' They just think you're acting weird for some reason and it makes them feel uneasy. If you are happy and relaxed and calm when you leave them, they will be too.

🐾 Don't punish OR reward. When you have left your dog and you come back, one of two things will have happened. The first is that he might have done something naughty, like had a poo or chewed the table leg, and the second is that he might have been good as gold and been happy and calm and just waited for you to come back. You need to ignore both these things and act exactly the same whatever has happened, no matter how hard it is! When you come back in, you can just give him a simple pat and a quiet and cheerful 'Good dog' or do something like take him out to go to the toilet if you've been gone for while. This way he isn't totally ignored and has something else to do.

Whatever you do as you come back into the room or the house will have no connection for your dog to what he has or hasn't done. It will just be what he learns to expect when you come back. Imagine your dad came into the room one day and totally ranted and raved at you about something you hadn't done and that you were totally unaware of. You would be bewildered and upset. It would make no sense to you and you might feel a bit worried the next time your dad came home, because you just couldn't tell what he was going to do or why. This is what it's like for dogs who get shouted at after they've done something bad. All it does is make them learn that your arrival is usually a bad thing and ruins your friendship.

Now, if you come back and your dog has been brilliant, of course you want to tell him what an amazing dog he is and how proud you are and give him loads of fuss. BUT this doesn't mean anything either, except that he will learn that you coming back is an incredibly amazing thing that's mega exciting. This might sound like a good idea but it doesn't help him stay calm and relaxed while you're gone. He'll start looking forward to you coming back SO much that he could get frantic waiting for it to happen and he'll still end up feeling upset that you're not there.

Humans try to do the right thing, but unless you understand what it says to the *dog*, you can get it badly wrong! Best to be calm and quiet when you leave and when you come back so that your dog will be just as relaxed as you. You'll often notice that the most highly strung, screechy owners have the most nervous, worried dogs and now you know why!

While we are talking about dogs and humans being friends, it's very important we look at the pestering from the other point of view. There are times that your dog may want to play when you are feeling too busy or tired. But what if you are the one pestering the dog? Dogs can't speak to us and tell us how they feel, but dogs are very good at communicating with their bodies. It's when humans don't notice what they are 'saying' that things go wrong. Learning how to 'speak dog' is very important to keep your dog happy and respect his needs but also to make sure you or your friends don't get hurt.

Lots of humans love to hug each other. We are an affectionate species. People love their pets, so our natural reaction is to hug our pets, dogs included. You might be surprised to learn that most animals *hate* being hugged. They find it really frightening and it makes them feel like they can't escape. Most dogs that let people hug them are doing it because they feel they have no choice. They *tolerate* it. Do you have a crinkly relative that your parents make you visit? Do they wear too much perfume and smell of talc? Do they always want to give you a big hug and a yucky, sloppy kiss?

Do you hate it but you know you have to do it, so you stand there frozen with a big fake smile on your face and wish for it to be over? That's what dogs are doing when owners (and sometimes strangers) hug them. Some dogs just can't tolerate it and sometimes they want to avoid humans all together. It's very important we let dogs have space and quiet time when they choose to.

Do you know who gets bitten by dogs more than anyone? It's children. Children love to be affectionate to animals, and see them as the great friends they are. The trouble is that children like to have close face-to-face time with their human friends, but animal friends don't really feel the same way. Some dogs are very affectionate and love to be stroked or have their ears rubbed or their bellies tickled, but you have to let them come to you. If you go to stroke them or play and they walk away, then you should leave them alone.

THE NEED TO BE WITH OR WITHOUT OTHER ANIMALS.

If a dog walks away from you and goes to its bed, you must NEVER follow it to try to get the stroke or the hug. This is the first way your dog is speaking to you and saying no thank you. If you keep trying, the dog will get as far away from you as he can, and if you keep following, eventually you will end up with the dog backed or curled into a corner or under a table leaning away from you. Next he will show you his teeth and might start growling, and if you still don't get the hint he might snap at you.

Even if it is just a warning nip, it can be painful and hurt you badly. Lots of people would think it was the dog's fault, but he tried to tell you SIX times to go away and leave him alone. If you ignored a friend telling you to stop doing something that many times, you wouldn't have any friends, would you? The other problem is that children are small and like to play face to face. This means when they have finally badgered the dog until breaking point, they usually have their face right in the dog's face and that's what gets bitten.

© iStock

© iStock

When a dog shows you his teeth, he wants you to go away.

When a dog tucks himself away, he wants to be left alone!

The gentlest dog in the world won't tolerate everything and they shouldn't have to. You wouldn't tolerate constant pestering from your brothers or sisters or your friends, so don't expect your dog to put up with it from you or your friends who come to visit. If you let your dog play and have attention when it suits both of you, but leave him alone when he's chosen to go away, you will be much better friends and he will love you much more. Remember, hugs don't say 'I love you' to a dog – space, trust and respect do.

Hang on a minute, this chapter is about the need to be with other animals, so we'd better have a look at that too because it is very important.

Pan and Badger. My best friends for fifteen years.

Doggy Friends!

Have you ever been really bored? Say it's the summer holidays and your friends are all off doing something with their families or on holiday or at a terrible summer camp or something. You ask your mum or dad to play with you. Depending on your age, this might be something like football, cards, a board game — you name it. Your mum or dad will be wanting to be good school-holiday parents, so they will make a special effort to give you extra time and attention. They probably feel a bit guilty about ignoring you for the last four weeks and telling you to play with your friends or your vile brother.

So you start playing and after a while you start to realise that your mum and dad aren't actually much fun, and after about twenty minutes more they start to get a glazed look on their face. You can tell their heart isn't really in it. The problem is that they are not *kids*. They might be the best *parents* in the world but playing with adults is not as much fun as playing with your friends. Adults are like a different, more boring species when it comes to fun. This is what it's like for dogs.

THE NEED TO BE WITH OR WITHOUT OTHER ANIMALS.

Now you and your family may well be the best dog *owners* the world has ever seen, but you are not dogs. Sure, you can throw a ball or try to play doggy games, but eventually you will get bored. You don't think you will, but you will. Some dogs would play every minute of the day if they could and humans just aren't up to it. Also we don't communicate like dogs, we don't play the same sorts of games as them, we're not as fast when we play chase and we never have as much energy as them. There are loads of reasons humans are a bit rubbish when it comes to playtime and, for that matter, rest time for dogs.

Humans just aren't the same when it comes to fun time...

When you see dogs properly playing it's absolutely brilliant to watch. Lots of people who only have one dog look really shocked when they see dogs play together. The dogs look really rough: there's teeth snapping, all sorts of weird and wonderful noises, they haul each other round by the neck, they try and nibble each other's legs to get the other one to fall over. Watching them play puts a guaranteed smile on your face whatever mood you were in.

© Marie Robertson

© Julie Irons

Normal play time can look really rough, but it's all fun for dog friends.

Even if you try your best, at some point your dog will nudge you for some affection, a stroke or a game and you will be busy. You might only be watching the TV, but you won't want to fuss the dog or play with him and he will eventually wander away and try and get someone else's attention. And probably fail.

Think back to their origins. Dogs are really social creatures that like to live with other dogs. So why do we keep so many on their own? If you have more than one dog, they always have each other. If they ever want to play, they can goad each other into it and are more likely to want to finish the game at the same time. They can share walks and smells and sights and sounds. When they are frightened they have the comfort of knowing there is another dog around. And when you do have to leave them for a little while, they are never alone. What could be better for any dog than the company and friendship of another dog 24/7?

Having one dog and looking after it REALLY well is quite a challenge, so if you're thinking of having more than one dog, you need to be very sure you can afford the time for exercise and training for both and of course have enough money.

If you do consider having more than one dog, try to avoid getting two puppies at the same time. Although they will be double cute, they can also be double trouble too. Puppies distract each other from training and it can be difficult to get them to learn how to behave round other dogs because they are so interested in each other. It's also worth thinking about having two dogs of different types as well as different ages. If they have different interests they are less likely to compete over things. If you had a sister or brother who liked exactly the hobbies as you, it might be hard not get too competitive about it! If you do get two puppies, perhaps because they desperately need a home, try to make sure they each have time alone for training and playing.

If you decide that one dog is best for you, try to think about people you know with dogs. Meeting other dog owners is a fun way to make friends for you and your dog. You and the dog get to have a friend at walk times and your dog can have some great doggy play as a bonus. A bit like you going out with your friends from school.

Now, taking on more than one dog might sound scary to some. Getting a dog in the first place is a massive commitment, as you will be finding out reading this book. BUT if you do everything you can to make sure you are a good owner and can afford to care for two dogs, in some ways it can be easier. They can be a little support unit for each other, they entertain each other in and out of the house and when you are not there you know they have each other.

Some dogs may be a bit wary of other dogs, but this is usually because they didn't meet enough dogs when they were little or maybe they had a bad experience. In the next chapter we're going to look at the biggest and most important thing when it comes to having happy dogs *and* being a happy owner. BEHAVIOUR! Humans are very good at getting this badly wrong. If everyone in the world who wanted a dog found out about dog behaviour beforehand, like you are, the adoption centres would soon be empty. Dog behaviour and human behaviour is really interesting and when you mix the two together you never really know what's going to happen. Best to make sure the ingredients are all perfect right from the start. Shall we begin?

Chapter 6

'What? I just found this lobster claw, I didn't do anything wrong.'

Now, have you ever had an itch in a place you couldn't reach? Right in between your shoulder blades, for example. You bend your arm right the way up your back but the tip of your thumb stops about a centimetre short of the itchy spot. Ooooohh, it drives you mad, doesn't it? You try and ignore it, but the more you try, the more you keep thinking about it, until you can't think about anything else. Eventually your mum finds you crazily scraping yourself up and down the door frame or discovers you have roped her best hairbrush to a wooden spoon and are frantically gouging it up and down your back with a weird look on your face like a cross between sheer panic and total heaven.

This is what it's like for animals who are not allowed to do the things they love or feel the need to do. It's the itch they can never scratch. All animals are born with some behaviours that are what's called 'innate'. This means they are born needing to do something even if they don't know why. Other behaviours are learnt as they grow. For example, an innate behaviour for children appears to be constantly picking your nose, whereas a learnt one is getting a tissue and actually wiping it!

Innate behaviours help animals get a head start, because they can do things without needing to be shown. One of the strongest and earliest innate behaviours you see is when animals suckle their mother's milk. Within minutes of being born, calves, lambs, kittens, puppies and human babies all start looking for their first warm drink of milk. They don't think about why and they don't need to, but it gives them a great start because they get a full tummy and lots of goodness straight away.

The important thing to remember is that even if we keep an animal in a way that means it doesn't *need* to do something any more, it will still feel the urge to do it. It will still be the itch they can't scratch. For instance wild dogs turn round

THE NEED TO EXPRESS NORMAL BEHAVIOUR.

in circles before they lie down, to flatten grass and hay and whatever they have made their den out of. We give dogs lovely comfy carpets and beds to sleep on but they still turn round in circles because it's an innate behaviour and they just can't help but do it.

This is where you'll realise how useful it is to have learnt everything we did about dogs in the wild and where pet dogs came from. Pet dogs may be more gentle and loving than their ancestors and their modern day cousins but they still have lots of the same instincts, fears and needs. A few thousand years of being pets doesn't beat out what millions of years of evolution has beaten in!

One of the biggest struggles owners have with dogs is behaviour. Unwanted behaviour is also one of the biggest reasons dogs get given away. Dogs pick up and learn their behaviour from life, their surroundings, their human and animal friends and what happens when they do certain things. It's easy to see how they can accidentally learn to misbehave if we don't get things just right.

Dogs are like toddlers. They can be loving and lots of fun and they can really make you laugh. They can also be difficult to understand, possessive, MEGA messy and they need very clear and consistent boundaries. As long as you know what's normal and how to encourage good behaviour, dogs are a fabulous addition to any family. As for toddlers — well, that's another story!

The easiest thing to do is look at what all dogs have in common when it comes to normal behaviour. Then we can think about different types of dog you might like and what's special to them and then most importantly what you and your family need to do to give your dog (and your family) the best chance to be happy.

What Normal Dogs Do

Poo, wee, whine, bark, howl, sniff each others' bums, chase animals, play, steal food, vomit and then eat it again, watch another dog vomit and then eat it, chew everything, bite, scratch, dig up your garden, shed hair, slobber, eat messily, bury toys in your sofa cushions, roll in fox poo, jump in muddy streams, shake the mud from streams all over you and your car, jump up at strangers, bark at the postman, bark at the door, bark at men in helmets, bark at passing cars and, of course, bark at the moon!

Normal dogs chase things...

...get muddy...

...get wet...

© Suzanne O'Neill

...find rank things to eat...

...sniff bums (even of other animals!)...

© Marie Robertson

...and dig big holes!

Not all dogs do all these things, but they are all normal behaviours and perfectly understandable even if we don't like some of them. They are left-overs from their wild roots. You can certainly train dogs not to do some of the things in this list, but some of these things you will have to accept and learn to love. To be honest, when one of your dogs clears up your other dog's sick before you've had a chance to, no matter how gross that is, it does save you a job!

It's really important to let animals be themselves as much as we can and do all the things they love and feel the need to do. When dogs aren't allowed to play or run or bark or have fun, they can feel really frustrated. One of the biggest mistakes humans keep making with dogs is punishing them for doing things that we don't like, rather than tackling the reason they might be doing the thing in the first place. For example, a dog that never gets walked and is left alone all day might destroy things in the house because the dog is SO unhappy, bored and lonely. Shouting at the dog when you come home because it has wrecked your coffee table isn't going to solve the reason it chewed the table, is it?! We all need to think about things from our pets' points of view sometimes. Dogs are always learning. Our job is to teach them the things we want them to do, rather than wait until they make a mistake. Imagine your first day at school. What if nobody told you which classroom to go to? As you wander around the school, everyone just shouts at you for being in the wrong place. How long might it take you to find your classroom, and how would you feel? It would be easier if someone just showed you the way to go. Owners need to show their dogs what to do and how to do it.

So, all animals have needs, and dogs are clever, social creatures that have lots of needs if they are to be happy. The happier your dogs are, the more likely they are to be good pets and great companions for you and your family, and you can be the great team that people and dogs have been for all those thousands of years. The main things that dogs need are company and being kept busy. Busy dogs surrounded by the people and dogs they love are the happiest, most relaxed dogs you'll meet. It's not difficult to make this happen, so let's look at how you can do it.

Choosing the Right Type of Dog for your Family

This sounds simple, but one of the reasons dogs end up in adoption centres is because people picked the wrong type of dog and thought it would just fit in around their lives. Different types of dog can be so different these days, they are almost like totally different animals. You must do your research before you decide, and you need to be honest about your family situation and how much time you have. Adopting a dog is always the best thing to do, and if you talk to an adoption centre, they can help find the right dog for your family, because that's what they are really good at. Talk to your local vet or vet nurse too. Hardly anyone asks us for advice before they get a pet, and we are the ones who can help so much, so please don't just look on the Internet. The more places you look for information, the more chance you'll have of getting a balanced and true view.

What you shouldn't do is pick a dog based on a film you've watched or because your favourite pop star has a certain one. When films like *Beethoven*, *101 Dalmatians* and *Sled Dogs* come out, people watch them and think, 'Ooh, I fancy having a St Bernard or a Dalmatian or a husky.' They go and buy, for example, a husky puppy, do no research at all and after a while they realise that huskies need to be exercised for virtually the whole day and can run hundreds of kilometres without even thinking about it and they are not suited to sitting in a flat in the centre of London! Or they get the big cuddly St Bernard puppy and about a year later they have a dog the size of a horse in their front room and it is slobbering all over the new baby! These dogs are destined for rehoming because their owners tried to do the right thing but for all the *wrong* reasons.

You need to think seriously about how active you are, how much space you have and how much time you have to play with, train, groom and exercise whatever type of dog you are thinking of.

Getting the Right Dog

All animals including humans have a period right at the start of their lives in which they learn about the world and all the weird and wonderful things that are normal in that world. This is called socialisation and it is absolutely essential to getting well-balanced, normal, relaxed and happy pets (and people!). If you get a puppy that has been born and lived in a dirty puppy farm cage, that has never met other dogs, people or anything that a normal house has in it, like noisy kids and scary machines like the Hoover and the television, you are very likely to end up with problems.

There are, sadly, lots of people who just want to make money out of selling as many cute puppies as possible and they know that people will see them, fall in love with them and take them, even if they are skinny and not well cared-for. If people keep buying from these places things will never get any better. Here are some ways to make sure you get a puppy that has been born, raised and cared for well;

- NEVER buy from a pet shop or any place that it is possible the dog was not raised in, like the motorway services! Online it can be very difficult to tell the good breeders from the bad, so be very careful. Always avoid adverts selling lots of different breeds.

- ALWAYS make sure you see the puppies' mother and, if possible, the father. Make sure they are friendly dogs and look well cared for.

- Download a copy of the AWF/RSPCA puppy contract. This is brilliant and comes with an information pack for the breeder to fill in and a contract for both of you to sign. The information pack helps you ask all the right questions about how healthy the puppies and the parents are and how well the dog has been socialised. It will help you find out about vaccinations and things like if the puppies and the mum have been properly wormed.

- If the breeder won't sign it or can't give you any of the information, walk away, no matter how much you've fallen in love! You won't be 'saving' a puppy, just making room for the next one to be badly cared for.

- Please, please, please always look in your local adoption centres before you think about buying a puppy. You may still find a puppy or you could get an older dog that may not be such a handful and might not need house-training. There are lots of beautiful dogs that need homes. Some centres like Battersea, Wood Green and Blue Cross are also very good at judging behaviour and can really help pick exactly the right dog for you and your family.

Stimulation

This is a fancy way of saying keeping your dog busy and interested. As well as their occasional quiet time, dogs need lots of mental and physical stimulation to stay happy. Just like kids! How long do you think you could sit in an empty room? Try it. Find the most boring room in your house, put a comfy cushion on the floor and see how long you can stay there. No TV, no books or devices or games or friends, no cheating! I'd be shocked if you managed half an hour. Dogs are the same. They can get easily bored and they need company. As we said in the last chapter, consider getting two dogs so they always have each other to play with and snuggle up to, but you still need to interact with them and play with them. When you get home from school you might be tired and want to veg out on the settee, but your dogs will be pleased to see you and want to play and go for walk and you need to be able to do that or think about a different pet. Think back to their wild relatives. They run miles and miles a day looking for food. Just because our dogs don't need to do that now doesn't mean they won't still want to run.

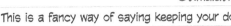

Dogs love to run ...

... and explore.

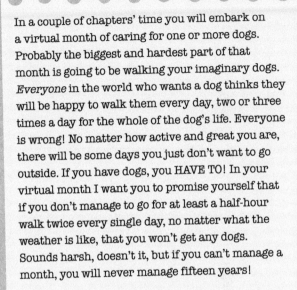

In a couple of chapters' time you will embark on a virtual month of caring for one or more dogs. Probably the biggest and hardest part of that month is going to be walking your imaginary dogs. *Everyone* in the world who wants a dog thinks they will be happy to walk them every day, two or three times a day for the whole of the dog's life. Everyone is wrong! No matter how active and great you are, there will be some days you just don't want to go outside. If you have dogs, you HAVE TO! In your virtual month I want you to promise yourself that if you don't manage to go for at least a half-hour walk twice every single day, no matter what the weather is like, that you won't get any dogs. Sounds harsh, doesn't it, but if you can't manage a month, you will never manage fifteen years!

There is a really excellent charity called the PDSA and every year they do a study into how well our pet dogs, cats and rabbits are cared for in the UK. In 2015 they found that over TWO MILLION dogs are left alone for more than five hours a day and that about a third of all dogs in the UK don't get let off their lead to have a run about. Please promise me this won't be you.

THE NEED TO EXPRESS NORMAL BEHAVIOUR.

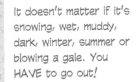

It doesn't matter if it's snowing, wet, muddy, dark, winter, summer or blowing a gale. You HAVE to go out!

It's good to play games at home and in your garden, but no matter how big your garden is, you must still take your dogs out and let them explore and have fun. Don't just wander to a nearby bit of grass and wait for them to have a poo, or go to the park and mindlessly throw a ball for them until they look exhausted. Enjoy it! Walking with dogs can be brilliant. It's good exercise for you and your family, it's a great way to explore new places and find beautiful outdoor spaces and woods and countryside, and watching dogs truly behave normally and enjoy themselves makes you feel GOOD. Dogs that are allowed to have lots of fun and play time will be happier, better pets.

Food for thought: everyone assumes dogs love to fetch. Some dogs have been bred to bring things back and lots of dogs do love to fetch a ball. BUT

1) hours of playing fetch is quite unnatural exercise for dogs and puts lots of strains on their joints with all the sudden stopping and twisting,

2) ball throwing is often used by humans as a lazy, quick way to make a dog look tired — this means the human doesn't feel guilty about not giving the dog a proper walk and can go home and put their feet up in front of the telly,

3) lots of dogs would be happy to run about and explore if we didn't perpetually throw balls for them, and

4) NEVER ever throw sticks for your dog. Every year dogs are seriously injured and killed by getting impaled on sticks.

So, occasionally playing ball may be fun but consider keeping the ball in your pocket for most of your walks so your dog's mind can go back to nature and he can enjoy sniffing and exploring the natural world around him. If he gets too carried away, producing the hidden ball can always remind him how interesting *you* are as well!

Training

A huge part of having a happy dog is having a dog that is well socialised and well trained. The bottom line is that if your dog is both these things, he can be allowed off his lead. If you can't trust your dog to ever get off his lead because he is vicious or scared or, simply and most importantly, because he won't come back to you, then you will never let him off and he will be miserable and annoying and pull you about and lunge at other dogs because he's really frustrated. There are two totally key things you need to do when you get your dog: good socialisation and recall.

DOG FACT:

It is possible to overdo the socialisation. Some owners let their dog play so madly with other dogs that they turn into a bit of a lunatic! Teaching your dogs a bit of control and to come back to you no matter how much fun they are having is really important.

THE NEED TO EXPRESS NORMAL BEHAVIOUR.

Training your dog to do little tricks can be fun for you and your dog. It's a good way to bond with them and it helps keep them occupied, focused on you and will help them be well behaved. Please don't treat them like circus animals though. Constant, serious obedience training or teaching them to do unnatural things like dancing about on their back legs isn't any fun for them and can be quite unpleasant.

So, go ahead and do fun training that both of you enjoy, but don't forget that the one command that you both need to absolutely nail is COME. You can pick any word you like, but having a dog that comes when it's called is pure magic. Just so you know, there is one word you can't pick and that is your dog's name. This may sound crazy but so many people shout their dog's name in all sorts of situations that the poor dog has no idea what it means. It could mean sit, come, wait, dinner time or 'OI, STOP THAT!'

You can think of any situation you like and the only word you need is 'come'. Your dog is running towards a road or towards an old, frail person or a frightened child or you need

to go home and he's been playing with his best dog friend for three hours. 'Come' sorts out every single one of those. Teaching your dog to come back to you is easy, but you need to work at it and be consistent and do it right from the start. Trust me, you will never regret it and it could save your friendship with your dog. A lot of other dog owners will be really jealous of you too because there are so many dogs that ignore their owners completely.

There's an easy way to get your recall and socialisation sorted and that is to go to a class. If you've got a puppy, talk to your vet or nurse. Most good practices will run puppy parties or socialisation classes. This is a great way to let your puppy meet other dogs, all ages of people, feel happy at the vets' and get training started. You can meet other people and dogs, and if you only have one dog, you might find people to walk with and your dog immediately gets a circle of doggy friends to have fun with.

Puppy parties are also good because it's a way you can get your puppy socialising with other dogs before they are allowed out properly, as the practice will make sure all the puppies are vaccinated.

If you have an older dog, or as your puppy grows, keep in touch with professionals like your vet or training class and keep the socialisation going with guidance. The sooner your dogs feel comfortable with all sorts of situations, the more chance you've got of having a happy little team, you included. The puppy contract and information pack I mentioned earlier also has a great section on things to think about to socialise your dog with. It's free to download to have a look at before you get a dog, and even if you're taking on an older dog, it's still full of useful information that might help you make decisions.

The last thing to say about training is about picking who gives you the advice. There are lots of people who call themselves trainers or behaviour specialists, who have no qualifications or rights to do so. Lots of people still think that dogs are like wolves and need to have a fierce pack leader. Some people even still think that it's OK to hit dogs, use spiky collars or electric shock collars to *make* dogs do what you want. This is totally unacceptable. All training should be about positive emotions and rewarding behaviour you want, not punishing behaviour you don't like. Remember, dogs are like kids. Would you rather your mum walloped you every time you made a mess, or gave you a little pocket money, a star on your chart or one of your favourite treats when you *cleared up* the mess you've made?

Either ask your vet to recommend someone or make sure the person you pick is actually a member of the APBC. This is the Association of Pet Behaviour Counsellors and is a great organisation of proper specialists with the most up-to-date knowledge and methods. These specialists are called 'clinical animal behaviourists' and can really help. If you have a dog whose behaviour is driving you mad, get it sorted out now, not next week or next month. Virtually all behaviour problems are perpetuated by humans not understanding why the dog is doing it and then reacting to it the wrong way. The longer you leave it, the worse it will get. You'll be amazed how quickly a good behaviour specialist can turn your life around and make your relationship with your dog what you had hoped it would be.

Life with dogs can be wonderful. You'll still have to put up with the hair and the toy-burying and the occasional snaffling of something rank, but if you know what's normal and accept it and you make the effort to let your dogs play, run, explore, learn and have company, then you've got a great chance of having the best years of your life with the best friends you'll ever have.

THE NEED TO BE PROTECTED FROM PAIN, INJURY AND DISEASE.

Every person and every animal gets poorly or hurt from time to time. That's just a simple fact of being alive. I always tell my daughters that their bumped shins and skinned knees are a good sign that they've been having plenty of fun. We already talked about what amazing machines bodies are, and one of their most amazing abilities is how they can heal and recover from injuries and disease. But you'll all know already that there are lots of illnesses and injuries that bodies can't cope with and that bodies need extra help with. It's not just about getting help for your pets when they are poorly or hurt: it's very important to find out all the ways you can stop them from getting ill in the first place.

We said before that dogs don't usually like being mauled about and cuddled all the time, but it is also important to make sure your dog is used to being handled for health reasons. You will need to check him over regularly to make sure he is healthy and he will need to go to the vet sometimes. If your dog is used to being carefully stroked and examined he will be less stressed and less likely to struggle and injure you, your vet or himself. If you get a puppy, you can get him used to being gently handled from a young age.

It's a good idea to go to your vet as soon as possible when you get your dog. He can have a good check over and you can watch and learn how to handle him best. If you are unsure, always get a grown-up to help you.

Let's look at things we can prevent first and then we can have a look at signs to watch out for that might mean your dog is under the weather.

Vaccinations

Depending on your age, you may or may not remember having your own vaccinations done. Having them done might involve the slight niggle of a jab, but they are one of the biggest life savers of recent times. Once humans started to understand how our bodies fight off diseases, we realised we could help out with some of the most horrible ones.

Your body and most animals' bodies have a super army inside them called the immune system. This army is made up of millions of cells, which are always on the lookout for bad bacteria and viruses. They never sleep, even when you do, and they happily lay down their lives to kill the bugs that try to make you poorly. You can think of these cells as your soldiers. They all have different ways of dealing with invaders. Some engulf the germs and eat them and some cells use bullets called antibodies. These soldier cells lurk round your body, and when they find an invader, they attack it. Now the first time they meet a new invader they won't have exactly the right sort of bullet to instantly get through the invader's armour, so usually it takes a lot of time and effort from the soldiers to try and overpower the invader and find out what their weakness is. For some nasty diseases the invaders are too strong and our immune cells can't win the battle and don't get the chance to make the right antibodies. These are the diseases which, especially in the past, make us and our pets really ill and even sometimes die.

Vaccinations give your soldiers super, armour-piercing bullets. Humans have studied the viruses and bacteria from many killer diseases. To make a vaccination they get some of the particular bug in a laboratory and they take away its weapons so it can't make you properly ill. The vaccine of weakened bugs is injected into you or given by your nose or mouth. Your soldier cells find the invaders without their weapons and they get the chance to examine their armour and work out how to design the right bullets or antibodies.

They kill the weakened intruders and they store away the design for the right antibody bullet. This means that when your body gets attacked by the real bug with all its weapons, your immune system is ahead of the game. Your soldier cells immediately make the exact bullet to get through their armour and it's game over before the war even begins. Millions and millions of humans and animals owe their lives to the power of vaccinations.

Different animals get different diseases, so they need very different vaccinations. This is why you need to find out all the facts for all the animals you're thinking about owning. There are quite a few vaccines your dog can have, but which ones they need will depend on where you live.

EVERY dog needs to be vaccinated against three very nasty diseases called distemper, parvovirus and adenovirus. And if you live in a country where rabies is a problem, they should also have a rabies vaccine. These diseases can make your dog very poorly and often die. Vaccination is essential to keep your dogs and everyone else's dogs safe and could also help get rid of these diseases altogether. Talk to your vet about what other vaccinations your dog will need.

Dogs and puppies need a course of two or three vaccinations the first time they have them. This ensures their soldiers make plenty of bullets and are absolutely certain about what the invaders' weaknesses are. After that your dog will need a booster vaccination every one to five years depending on the vaccine. These must be done to remind the soldiers what to do. These visits to the vet are also excellent because your dog will get a really good health exam, you can get your vet to make sure they are not too fat or thin and you can find out if there is anything new you should know about.

Neutering

Neutering is when your pet has an operation to make sure he or she can't have any babies. This is important to help reduce the number of unwanted or neglected pets. A lot of people don't have their animals neutered early enough and they end up having accidental babies that could end up without homes and without anyone to feed or care for them.

Being neutered not only stops unwanted babies but it also helps keep animals healthy because it prevents some diseases like certain infections and some types of cancer.

Talk to your vet about when to have your dog neutered and what you need to do to help your dog get well soon after her trip to the surgery. If you're adopting a dog, he or she will probably already be neutered. If she or he is too young, most adoption centres will include the cost of the neutering in the adoption and you can get it done when your dog is old enough. Once it's done, your dog has a much better chance of being happy and healthy for longer.

Parasites

Parasites are little creatures that live in and on other animals. All animals and humans come into contact with parasites. It's just a fact of life. It doesn't mean you're dirty or bad in some way, it just shows how brilliant parasites are at hitching a ride on the animals they like best. You probably will have heard of the most common parasites: fleas, worms, mites and lice.

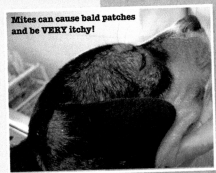

Mites can cause bald patches and be VERY itchy!

All parasites are annoying but some can be very dangerous and some can also pass from animals to humans, so it's very important to make sure you know all about the ones your pet could get. Your vet will be able to tell you about the most important ones where you live and which treatments are safe and effective to use for your pet.

Worms and fleas are very common in dogs, so let's say a little about them.

Mites like this one are so tiny you can only see them with a microscope

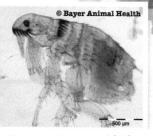

© Bayer Animal Health

Fleas can be seen with the naked eye but spend most of their time off your pet, so can be difficult to find!

Fleas

Anyone who says their dog doesn't get fleas is wrong. Fleas can't fly but they are some of the best jumpers in the world. They live in the undergrowth and grass and also in your carpets, bedding and furniture at home. They hop onto your dog when they are hungry and bite them to drink their blood. After their meal they hop off again and lay eggs in your house. For every flea you see on your pet, there will be a hundred in the house. Yikes!

Fleas are annoying because they cause itching, but some dogs are allergic to the bites and can be so itchy they tear themselves to pieces and can get infected skin and bald patches. Fleas can also spread diseases and worms, so they can be a massive problem. They can also bite humans.

Luckily, once again we live in a time where we can get rid of fleas easily and also prevent them from getting a hold in the first place. Use what your vet recommends and keep your treatments up to date and you can ensure your house and dog never get infested!

Worms

Worms (parasites, not the type you find in your garden!) live in your dog's intestines and around the body, so you usually won't know they are there. They lay their eggs there, which come out in your dog's poo and either get swallowed again when your dog grooms itself or get left in the garden or out on walks to infect other animals. Some worms are just trouble because they take your dog's food from the inside, but other worms can cause lots of internal damage as well. The signs of one type of worm called lungworm can be difficult to spot because it causes so many problems. These worms can wiggle and wander in lots of different places in your dog's body and how poorly your dog is will depend on what the worms are doing. Lungworm, like some other types of worm around the world, can even kill dogs.

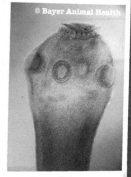

© Bayer Animal Health

Close-up views of the worms that can live inside our pets

© Bayer Animal Health

As with so many things, prevention is always better (and easier!) than cure, so it's very important you treat your dog to kill and prevent worms by following your vet's advice.

Some worms that dogs carry can pass to humans and can cause serious damage when they wiggle and travel around inside *your* body. Children are the most likely people to catch these worms from parks and places like that because they have more fun than adults and don't just stand around with their hands in their pockets! This is why it is SO important to pick up your dog's poos when you are out and about. Not only does it keep the towns and countryside smelling fresh and looking nice, but it stops worms from spreading, which is much more important.

These days there are quite a few medicines that treat fleas and worms all at the same time to make life easy. You can even get apps which remind you when to do it. Always talk to your vet about what to use and make sure you are using something that is safe for the size of dog you have.

© Bayer Animal Health

Lungworm can show up in lots of ways and can be fatal. It is definitely best prevented.

THE NEED TO BE PROTECTED FROM PAIN, INJURY AND DISEASE.

Microchipping

This isn't a disease, but is a good thing to do when you get a dog. Microchips are tiny things about the size of a grain of rice that get implanted under the skin of your pet. Every chip has a different number on it and this gets registered to your details. This way if your pet goes missing it can be scanned with a little microchip reader and you can be re-united with your pet really quickly. Although by law in many countries dogs have to have a collar with a name and number on it, collars can come off. Having a microchip is the safest and surest way to make sure your pet comes back to you if it gets lost. It's a quick and easy thing to do, so have a chat with your vet about it. You might find it's actually the law to have your dog microchipped: it is in the UK, and you should find out about where you live. Whether it's the law or not, it just makes good sense!

Obesity

We said all the way back in Chapter 3 how bad obesity is. Being too fat has been proved to shorten life, so if you'd like to have your lovely dogs as long as possible, remember to keep them slim. Being too fat puts lots of strain on the heart and joints and can make life really hard for dogs. Dogs don't sweat like humans and they rely on panting to cool down in hot weather. Being too fat can make this almost impossible and can also make dogs feel very frustrated if they can't run about and play.

© PDSA

A very fat dog that can't run about...

Most dogs get too fat because they are fed too much or get given fatty human foods that aren't right for them. But sometimes dogs also get too fat because of guilt. Owners love to treat their dogs, and if they are busy and don't have time to walk them, they make themselves feel less guilty by giving the dog a nice treat instead. This is totally the wrong thing to do. Not only does the dog get extra calories it doesn't need: it doesn't get enough exercise either. No wonder they get fat! Food isn't the only thing dogs enjoy. As we said, they enjoy company and stimulation too. There are lots of ways to show your dogs how much you love them besides giving them food.

© Susannah Coleman

...compared to a beautifully slim, active one.

A very easy way to keep in the right habits from the start is to have a no-scavenging rule. There are lots of families who spend their whole lives with a salivating dog staring at them the whole time they are eating or making food. This is horrible for everyone concerned, including the dog who is constantly looking for food and titbits. If you never feed your dogs from the table or when you are eating or preparing food, they will never expect it and so won't do this behaviour. They will know when it is their mealtimes. You can feed your dog 2, 3 or even 4 times a day if you want to. Just remember to split their whole ration over these meals, don't feed them extra.

If even one person in the family sneakily gives the dog treats from the table, he'll get into bad habits that might be difficult to break. You're not being cruel by not feeding your dog your own food or every time you eat, but letting your dog get obese is just as cruel as starving him, so be good right from the start!

Stick to good rations of the right food, make sure you know what body condition your dog is and if you are ever unsure just ask. Your vet or vet nurse will always be happy to help you if you think your dog is getting too fat. If you already have a fat dog, it's not too late. There are special diets your vet can get for you to help your dog lose weight safely. Remember the very fat dog from the start of this section? Well, here she is after a good diet...

© PDSA

Amazing! Doesn't she look fantastic?

Cartoon Dogs and Funny Fur!

As we said when we looked at where dogs came from, humans have bred dogs of different shapes and sizes. To start with, this was for a reason, to help us do certain jobs. Lots of dogs still work for humans now, like sniffer dogs, sheep dogs and guard dogs. Over time we've started having dogs just as pets, but people have carried on inventing more and more breeds. The problem is that some breeds have become very odd shapes compared to a 'normal' dog shape and in recent years these shapes have become more and more extreme. Some are so extreme they actually look like the old cartoons of themselves.

It's not really anything to laugh about though. Nature took millions of years to perfect the shape of dogs, wolves and other canids. Evolution made sure that they could run, breathe, hunt, play, see, hear and smell. Their legs are straight and strong, their bodies are in proportion, they have long muzzles and strong teeth and open, clear eyes and ears. They have short, easy fur and good skin and the ones that live in cold climates have thick fur, not extremely long fur.

© iStock

© iStock

© iStock

Wild canids have long, straight legs, short fur, clear eyes and ears and long muzzles.

THE NEED TO BE PROTECTED FROM PAIN, INJURY AND DISEASE.

Then humans interfered and as usual we didn't think about what we were doing. I'm very sad to say that inbreeding of our beautiful dog friends and the shapes we've made some breeds have caused lots of disease and health problems. When you're thinking about what sort of dog to get, bear in mind that in general, cross-breeds are healthier than pedigrees. I don't mean fancy, 'designer' cross-breeds; I mean good old mongrels where you can't really tell what breed they might be. If you do want a certain breed, ask your vet about the healthiest options rather than picking a fashionable or quirky breed. As we said before, have a good look round an adoption centre. You will probably find a dog to fall in love with that you weren't expecting at all.

Here are some extremes of shapes and characteristics and what they mean to the dog, that you might want to think about (and avoid) when you are picking your dog.

🐾 Flat faces. Breeds with flat faces can have breathing problems, may not be able to exercise and can struggle to cope with the heat because they have funny airways. They can also have eye problems because of bulging eyes or eyelids that roll in and rub their eyes all the time. Lots of owners of flat-faced dogs think it's cute that the dogs snore. In fact, it just means they can't breathe properly. Not very cute at all!

© David Gould

Flat faces can mean breathing problems, skin and eye problems.

🐾 Very wrinkly skin. This is not natural at all and can cause painful skin infections in the folds. Dogs that have really droopy skin on their face can also have problems with their eyes because their eyelids are all droopy.

Skin wrinkles cause pain and infection.

© David Gould

Droopy eyes don't work properly and get damaged.

© iStock

🐾 Very long hair or no hair. Dogs can manage with very long fur but it can take a lot of work from you to keep under control and it can be unpleasant for the dogs. Dogs with very long fur can struggle with the heat and it also makes it difficult for them to stay clean and also to 'talk to other dogs'. Dogs use subtle things like eye contact and making the fur on their shoulders stand up if they are in a certain mood. Very long haired dogs can't do this and their eyes are hidden, so life can be hard. If you want to give a very long-haired dog a home, have him regularly clipped short to keep him happy. On the other hand some breeds of dog are almost bald. These can be prone to cold, sunburn and skin injuries and should be avoided.

Very long hair is best avoided or kept short by regular clipping.

© iStock

Even dogs with thick fur like our Pan are much happier clipped in the summer.

Hairless dogs should be avoided.

© iStock

Chapter 7

🐾 Very long, hairy or dangly ears. Dogs with ears like this can be really miserable, prone to ear infections and get ears clogged up with hair and wax.

© iStock

People think it's funny to see ears like this, but it is definitely no joke for the dog.

If you're worried, talk to your local vet, do your research and also just think back to nature. If you pick a dog, large, medium or small, that is roughly the same *shape* as those wild cousins, you will have a good chance of a healthy friend. Just avoid the weird and wonderful extremes, no matter how quirky or fashionable they are.

🐾 Short legs and very long backs. Dogs with little legs and long backs like 'sausage dogs' can have weak backs and can have problems that mean they can't walk.

🐾 Giants and tea-cup dogs. Very huge dogs and very tiny dogs both have different problems of their own. Giant dogs are prone to bad hearts and joints and may not live long at all. Tiny dogs can be very fragile and can have bad teeth, skull problems and poor joints among other things.

🐾 Some breeds of dog are prone to problems inside that you can't see, like joint problems, allergies, cancer and heart problems. Make sure you find out about any breed you are thinking of and what diseases they are most likely to get.

© iStock

© iStock

Aim for a natural dog shape rather than a cartoon!

© iStock

© iStock

Is Your Dog Healthy?

The things we've mentioned so far are the big things to be aware of when it comes to having and choosing a pet dog, but there are all sorts of other diseases, conditions and injuries that can happen. If you want to learn about every single one, then you should do your homework, work hard and become a vet, because I haven't got room for all of it here! The best way to keep your pets healthy in general is to be observant and know what's normal so you can spot when things are wrong. Kids are usually way better at noticing things than grown-ups, so put yourself in charge of keeping a watchful eye on the dog!

If you are ever worried, take your dog to the vet. Your vet won't think you're silly if there's nothing wrong. It's always better to be safe than sorry.

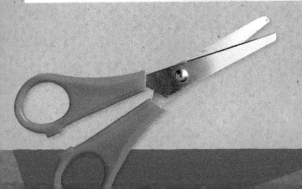

Things to watch for in your dog themselves

🐾 **Bright eyes** No runny eyes or discharge, no swelling round the eyelids or redness. Poorly eyes can be because of infections or scratches or even problems elsewhere in the body and should always be checked out.

🐾 **Clean nose** No snot or mucus coming from either side, no frequent sneezing or rubbing at the face. Don't worry if your dog's nose isn't cold and wet all the time. It's a bit of an old wives' tale that they need to be cold and wet.

🐾 **Shiny, healthy fur** Look out for bald patches, redness and scabs. You don't often see fleas, but sometimes if you see lots of little black dots in the fur this could be flea poo. It's a great Detective Clue to find. If you are ever unsure whether it is dirt or flea poo, there's a great trick you can do. Comb the specks onto a white piece of kitchen or loo roll. Add some water. If it's dirt, nothing will happen, but if it's flea poo it will turn into a red smudge because flea poo is made of blood. You can amaze and horrify your parents all in one go! Dogs can get itchy for lots of other reasons too, like mites, lice and allergies. If your dog seems itchy all the time, get him checked out.

🐾 **Comfortable, clean ears** If your dog's ears seem dirty or itchy or you see her keep shaking her head, she could have ear mites, something trapped in the ear, like a grass seed, or allergies. Time for a trip to the vet.

Chapter 7

THE NEED TO BE PROTECTED FROM PAIN, INJURY AND DISEASE.

Things to watch for in your dog themselves

- **Body Condition Score, or BCS** As we said, it's really good to understand body condition. It's a way of talking about how fat or thin your animals are. The scale is 1 to 5, where 1 is dangerously thin, 3 is normal and 5 is dangerously obese. Keeping your dog in the right body condition is essential for good health.

- **Make sure your dog's nails are not overgrown** Most dogs never need their nails trimmed, because they get worn down by walking, running and digging. Old dogs sometimes need a trim, or if you have a dog that can't exercise for some reason. If you're ever worried, get your vet to have a look. Don't try to trim dogs' nails yourself, because you can make them bleed and really hurt them.

- **Healthy gums and clean teeth** Your vet will always check your dog's teeth when he has his boosters, but if you notice really stinky breath or if your dog yawns and you see the teeth are brown, get them checked over. It's best if you can get into the habit of brushing your dog's teeth from the start. Just like us, it will help keep his teeth healthy and strong. Don't use human toothpaste: it's designed to be spat out. Your vet or nurse will be happy to show you the best way to get started.

- **Lumps and bumps** If you find a lump or bump, take your dog to the vet. They can be lots of different things from fatty lumps to tumours. Most are nothing to worry about, so don't panic, but get them checked to be safe.

© PDSA

Body condition score

1 Very thin
- Very little muscle
- Easily seen ribs, backbone and hipbones
- No body fat

2 Underweight
- Clearly seen ribs and backbone
- A little fat over hipbones
- Obviously tucked-in waist

3 Ideal
- Can feel ribs, backbone and hipbones, but not prominent
- Smooth, curved, tucked-in waist
- Base of tail smooth

4 Overweight
- No waist and back broader
- Ribs, backbone and hipbones difficult to feel
- Fat at base of tail

5 Obese
- Bulging pot belly
- Cannot feel ribs, backbone or hipbones
- Thick fatty pads at base of tail

pdsa.org.uk

pdsa HELP A VET HELP A PET

Always aim to have a number 3!

Things to watch for in your dog themselves

🐾 **Look out for odd behaviour** This could be anything from being 'a bit quiet', straining to go to the toilet, not moving around as normal, sneezing, coughing or panting all the time. Basically anything out of the ordinary. If you see any weird or unusual behaviour, get your dog to the vet as soon as you can.

🐾 **Normal appetite and thirst** This is the amount your dog normally eats and drinks. Often in dogs one of the first signs of problems are changes in appetite or thirst. This could be more or less, so it's very important once again to know what's normal. If you do notice any changes in eating or drinking amounts, off to the vets you go...

Things To Watch For In Your Dog's Surroundings

🐾 Normal faeces (poo) and urine (wee) If you notice problems like blood in the wee or your dog only manages to pass drips and drops of wee, you need to go to the vet straight away. Diarrhoea is also a definite sign that all is not well. Once again, you'll soon get used to what's normal for your dog. If you don't look, you don't know!

🐾 Vomiting Most dogs, like children, are sick very occasionally. Sometimes they eat something disgusting or get a bug. If your dog vomits for more than half a day or there's blood in it, it's important to take them to the vet or give your vet a ring. Vomiting can make your dog dehydrated and really ill if she doesn't get better quickly. It's better to be safe than sorry.

Don't panic about all these things: the more you get to know your dog, the sooner and more easily you'll spot the odd things. The better an owner you are, the healthier your dog will be and hopefully the fewer trips to the vet you'll need. Remember that even though most dogs are pretty healthy animals, usually you can't just get one and forget about them. Be observant and if in doubt, always ask your vet; that's why we're there!

Now you have all the facts about where dogs came from and you know how to keep your pet dogs happy as well as healthy. So it must be time for even more fact-finding, some virtual reality and some good old maths. Basically it's time to actually answer that crucial question:

Are dogs the right pet for me and my family?

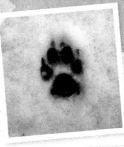

In this chapter we're going to crunch some numbers and you're going to have to start investigating facts from some other places besides this book. We're also going to embark on a virtual month of being a dog owner. You might feel silly but it's a brilliant way of checking if you actually do have what it takes to be a dedicated owner of a dog. You can do it all by yourself or you can involve the whole family in the decisions, care and sums.

If you find yourself, towards the end of the virtual month, getting a bit bored with pretending to play with, feed, train and walk a teddy every day, remember this: a well-cared-for dog can live well over *fourteen* years, so you need to get used to it!

Week One — Walking and *How Much??!*

Now, if you've read any of the other books in this series you might know that usually you don't have to do all the jobs at the same time until the last week of this practice month. BUT there are so many dogs in the world that never get walked or don't get *enough* exercise that I want you do this part every single day of the whole month. If, between you and your family, you can't manage at least two walks of half an hour (and preferably more) a day, then you're not going to manage years and years. Walking dogs in the rain, cold and dark is sometimes not very nice and it feels a bit inconvenient sometimes. But remember, you can't deprive an animal of one of its needs because it is inconvenient. If you want a dog, you have to go OUTSIDE! You can have a rota or take it in turns as long as it gets done.

On the next page is a box to fill in. It's a good idea to write in how long your walk was in time or distance. If one of you has a smartphone, you could map your walks and make it more interesting. If you get a puppy, you won't need to do much walking to start with, but for this month we are going to pretend your dog is a grown-up with all its exercise needs. Depending on what type of dog you get, the times will vary. I think you should aim for at least thirty minutes at least twice a day. If you can manage an hour one or both times a day, then well done you. Use this time to think about how accessible good walks are where you live and whether you will need to be driven somewhere for an interesting walk. Travel time is on top of walk time...

Day	Monday	Tuesday	Wednesday	Thursday	Friday	Saturday	Sunday
Walk am.							
Walk pm.							

Besides the walking, we'll spend the first week finding out some costs, to ease you into it gently. Some of these costs are definitely a one-off, like neutering. Things like buying bowls and beds might seem like that too, but bear in mind that over ten to fifteen years, lots of things might wear out and need replacing, so a bit of reserve is always needed. Things like toys are good to rotate or renew, so try to get an idea of the cost of say three average toys and allow that amount every month or so.

Now is also the time to consider right from the outset what sort of house or flat you live in and the area it's in. If you've already decided you can't give a dog the best place to live, then you might not need to go much further and can avoid the painful maths! So, assuming you think you can provide the right environment for a dog, here's a place to start filling in those numbers. The boxes that are coloured in green are either one-off costs or costs that will only need to be rarely repeated. This will help you and your family get an idea of how much your initial outlay is likely to be compared to ongoing costs. Don't forget, though, that virtually everything will need to be paid for at the start, so add everything together for your start-up costs!

Things to find out from the pet shop/adoption centre or the internet

Item	Cost £
The dog! Bear in mind that adoption centre costs may include neutering, vaccinating and microchipping. If you're planning to have two dogs or puppies, remember to multiply this by two. Remember too that just because a particular breed is mega-expensive, it doesn't mean it's better than a mongrel!	
Brush for grooming.	
Bowls for food and water for each dog.	
Bed for each dog. These should only need replacing occasionally but some dogs will chew their beds, so you never know.	
Collars and leads/harness for each dog. If you get a puppy, you'll need to replace these as they grow.	
Good-quality food. Talk to a vet before you get your dog. Find out the cost of a bag of dry food or tray of tins and try to estimate how much you'll need each month and the cost.	
Puppy/dog crate. These are great for helping with house-training but also give your dog somewhere to go if they'd like to be alone. Talk to your vet, nurse or behaviourist for how to use them. They are not supposed to be dog prison!	
Poo bags. You need to get used to always having several poo bags in your pocket. You don't want to get caught out!	
Toys. Get an idea of how much toys cost to allow for occasional replacements.	
A secure garden. Have a chat with your parents about whether your garden is secure and what you might need to do to stop a little puppy or a big dog escaping.	
Total	

Things to find out from your vet

Procedure	Cost £
Microchipping. Depending on where you live, this may well be compulsory.	
Neutering. This will be different for males and females so make sure you find out both.	
Vaccination. Find out what vaccines your dog will need and how often each of the boosters is due.	
Pet insurance. Per month or per year. Ask your vet to recommend a company because some policies can let you down.	
Flea and worm treatment. Cost per month.	
Average consultation cost if your dog gets poorly.	
Total from this and the last page added together	

These numbers may be a bit mind-bogglingly big when you look at them, but that's why I wanted you to do it. There is no such thing as a cheap pet. Obviously you will have worked out that once you're all set up your monthly costs may be much more manageable, but don't forget about vets' fees and unexpected problems. The brilliant charity the PDSA produce a report every year called the PAW report, which looks at how animals are cared for in the UK. They estimate that dogs can cost up to a massive £30,000 in a lifetime, so you need to be prepared!

Week Two — Walking and handle with Care

This week, besides those all-important walks, you are going to spend time and energy devoted to your new (pretend!) dog and getting to know it. It's important to get your dog used to being handled right from a young age if possible. As we said in the last chapter, this will help them feel safe and secure with you and not feel threatened. If they are happy being handled gently, they will be much less likely to be frightened of you and also less likely to hurt themselves thrashing and kicking to get away from you. It will also make them feel less stressed when they need to go to the vet and be handled by strangers. Remember not to overdo it. It's not about hugging and mauling. Just try to get them used to gently looking in their ears and mouths, running your hands all over their bodies and picking up their feet to gently check their paws. Ask an adult to help you or your vet or vet nurse to show you if none of you are sure.

Remember when you first get a dog that you need to let her come to you, and to stay calm and quiet around her. Never chase her or grab her or she will not trust you.

Hopefully if you've picked your dog or puppy wisely or got an adoption centre to do that work for you, then you will have a friendly, sociable and happy dog who will soon be ready to play and come for fuss, but be prepared for the fact it might take time. All animals vary and your dog might not be interested in fuss from you. If they are like this, remember to respect their needs and be happy just to watch them and enjoy their company when it suits both of you.

Being around pets is as much about really good observation as it is about handling and training. Kids are way more observant than most grown-ups. Use this week to think about what you've learnt about dog behaviour. If you do get a dog, you need to learn what is normal for your dog. How he moves, how much he eats and what his favourite activities and games are. How much does he seem to drink most days or how much water disappears from the bowls? How much time does he spend exploring and sleeping? The more you notice these things and are observant, the better an owner you'll be, because you'll immediately see when something is different.

When your dog does come for fuss, when you're playing together or when you are handling him, remember to look out for possible health problems. Black dirt, which might be a sign of fleas, bald patches, limping, bad breath, lumps, bumps, clumps of fur or sneezing and runny eyes. Play games with your dog, make training fun. Playing together and learning things together is a great way to bond with your dog and become great friends. The more active your dog is, the healthier and slimmer he will be and the less bored and frustrated. Talk to your vet about how much exercise your particular dog needs for his age. Too much too young can cause problems, so make sure you find out.

Here is a table to fill in for this week. Once you are in the swing of things you'll find that most of the observation just becomes second nature. It's not really like rabbits and guinea pigs, where you need to go to their cage and handle and check them twice a day. Dogs are easier in some ways because you'll be sharing your home with them so will see them a lot, but still keep in mind that you can't just forget about them. If you do plan to have dogs kept outdoors, you will have to make time to go to them and do these checks. You'll probably need to set aside a good hour of your day at least to make sure you do these things right. There's also grooming to think about. Depending on the type of dog you get, this might be a daily job or a weekly job. You'll need to do it more at certain times of the year too, so it's important to find time now to do it. Oh yes, and don't forget to wash your hands after you've been stroking, grooming or handling your dog.

Job/Day	Monday	Tuesday	Wednesday	Thursday	Friday	Saturday	Sunday
Walk am.							
Walk pm.							
Grooming. We'll say half an hour three times a week for practice.		x		x	x	x	
Time nearby, stroking and gentle handling.							
Play time and training. Be inventive and have fun with your dog while he learns.							
Any sign of problems? Time for observation.							

Week Three — Walking and What Goes In Must Come Out!

This week you'll be doing the dirty work! Besides walking you'll be feeding and checking the water is fresh and clean. In the table I have put two mealtimes down. If you have a puppy, she might need four or five meals a day, so this will vary with your dog's age. Lots of people only feed their dogs once a day. There's no rule, but I have always fed my dogs two or three meals a day because I think it is fairer and better for them. Have a chat with your vet about what they recommend.

It's a rare person who *really* enjoys cleaning anything, so you can be forgiven for not looking forward to this, but it is a huge part of pet keeping. There is no getting away from the fact that some of what goes in has to come out and it is up to you to clear it up! Handling poo and sometimes wee can make you poorly, so you need to make sure you know all about hygiene. Picking up your dog's poos is totally essential. Not only is it the law in most places, but it stops the spread of worms and diseases and keeps our environment much nicer. When you're out on walks you'll do this as you go along, but your dog might also poo in your garden. You'll need to let your dog in the garden last thing at night to give her a chance to go to the toilet, just like we like to do at bedtime. You'll soon find that your garden can get pretty gross, so you need to check for poos in the garden every day and clean them up.

Of course you still don't have a dog, so this week is about setting aside the time you need as if you had to do these jobs. Why not get your mum or dad to give you a boring or yucky job to do that would take about the same amount of time? Clean the bathroom *including the toilet*, empty all the bins or do the ironing. You'll get an idea of the more boring side of being a pet owner and you'll get massive brownie points at the same time.

Checklist for this week

Job/Day	Monday	Tuesday	Wednesday	Thursday	Friday	Saturday	Sunday
Walk am.							
Walk pm.							
Feed am.							
Feed pm.							
Wash food bowls.							
Clean water bowls and give fresh water am.							
Check/freshen water and clean bowls if necessary pm.							
Check garden for poo and clean up.							
Check toys and replace if necessary (once a week).	X	X	X	X	X	X	

Week Four — EVERYTHING, Including Walking of Course!!

And now for the grand finale. This week you will need to find a few hours every day in your hectic schedule to devote to your new pet. Fill in the rather large table below and add in your ongoing costs at the bottom. Most of all try to enjoy it, because if you do get a dog, you're going to be doing this for years, not weeks, and probably until you leave home!

Job/Day	Monday	Tuesday	Wednesday	Thursday	Friday	Saturday	Sunday
Walk am.							
Walk pm.							
Grooming. We'll say half an hour three times a week for practice.		X		X	X		X
Time nearby, stroking and gentle handling.							
Play time and training. Be inventive and have fun with your dog while he learns.							
Any sign of problems? Time for observation.							
Feed am.							
Feed pm.							
Wash food bowls.							
Clean water bowls and give fresh water am.							
Check/freshen water and clean bowls if necessary pm.		X		X			X
Check garden for poo and clean up.	X	X	X	X	X	X	
Check toys and replace if necessary (once a week)	X	X	X	X	X	X	
Costs £							

Time for the Family Debate

Over the last few weeks and having read the rest of the book, you should now have some idea of what keeping a dog is actually about. If you're like most people, you'll probably be quite shocked. It's very rare for people to realise just how much time and money is needed to look after pets well. Anyone can look after pets badly, but I hope that now you will most definitely not be one of them! You've probably been talking to your family about things as you've gone along, but if not, now is the time to do that. You can call a meeting and present your facts, like all the best detectives do. Because now you really do have everything you need to answer that question. **And to answer it honestly.**

Well? I'm listening. What's the answer?

Things you might want to talk about at your family meeting

🐾 If you are under sixteen someone else in your family will be legally obliged to provide all these things for your dog and they need to agree to that!

🐾 Does a dog, from what you've learned, tick the boxes of what you'd like in a pet? If you thought they were something different, don't be ashamed to change your mind. That's the whole point of finding out all about them – to make the right choices.

🐾 Can your family afford the costs you've found out? Lots of people get embarrassed talking about money, but now is not the time to be shy. If you can't afford it, don't get one.

🐾 Did you have the time, energy and room to provide for all the things your imaginary pet needed? And if so, could you do that for about fifteen years? If you're over the age of about five, you may well be moving on before your dog dies, so your family will need to carry on where you leave off. Are they willing to do that?

🐾 Is the whole family on board with the idea?

I hope that after all your hard work you finally get the answer you wanted, but what about if you didn't? Time to ask the next question: What if the answer is no?

Chapter 9

As we said all the way back in Chapter 1, you shouldn't really ask yourself what sort of pet you want: you should ask yourself what sort of pet you can care for properly. The fact-finding you've done up to now will hopefully have helped you work out if a dog is an animal you can keep healthy and, just as importantly, happy. As I said at the end of the last chapter, there is absolutely no shame in finding out that the answer is no. That is the point of your mission and the book, to help you and your family make the right and responsible choice. Not only will you have happy pets, but hopefully you'll have pets that make you happy too. Very often pets get given away because they were bought on an impulse with no research. In the case of a dog, it can easily happen too. If kept alone or mauled about, they can be very unfriendly and unhappy animals and not very nice pets through no fault of their own, simply because they are misunderstood and poorly cared for. The vicious circle starts and soon you've got a lonely, bored, frustrated dog wrecking the house and soon given away.

What if the answer is 'No dogs'?

So if you have done your numbers and learnt your facts and decided that a dog is not the right pet for you or your family, then that is just as worthwhile as deciding to go ahead and get one. A massive well done either way. You should be very proud of yourself. If you found that a dog didn't tick your boxes or you couldn't tick theirs, it doesn't necessarily mean you can't have a pet; we just need to look at some alternatives, depending on what you were struggling with.

The brilliant animal charity we mentioned before called the PDSA have come up with a great way to think about having pets, and that is to think PETS! That is: Place, Exercise, Time and Spend. Going through these four things for whichever animal you are thinking about is a good way to decide if you can keep them properly. On their website they have a great tool to help people find the right pet for their own situation, so do have a look at that as well. For now we'll go one step at a time through PETS and see what other pets might suit you best! Remember that this is just a pointer. You will still need to thoroughly research any pet you are thinking of. Just because one animal may need less room or be cheaper to keep, there may be other things about it that might put you or your family off.

Chapter 9

WHAT IF THE ANSWER IS NO?

Place

A dog will share your house or garden, but you still need to think about how big your house is and how easy or hard it was in your virtual month to give your dog enough exercise. For example, if your were thinking of getting a dog that needs miles and miles of exercise every day but you need to drive twenty miles to find any open space, you need to think again. So what about the alternatives?

Rabbits and guinea pigs.

These can make great pets but in lots of ways are harder to keep than a dog. Rabbits and guinea pigs need a lot more space than most people imagine. You can't just buy a hutch and forget about them. They need really big hutches and exercise areas whether they're indoors or out. Having said that, if you can't have a dog because you don't have anywhere nearby to go for good walks, you might find rabbits or guinea pigs a better option. You can build or give them a big, secure, fun place in your garden or house if you have enough room at home.

Other 'small furries'.

Small furries are things like rats, mice, hamsters and gerbils. Some of these certainly need less space than a dog and would definitely be worth considering. There are some more exotic small furries kept as pets these days, like chinchillas and degus, but some of these need pretty huge cages to let them express all their behavioural needs, so be very careful to do your research before you decide.

Cats.

Lots of people say you are either a dog person or a cat person so you might not like the idea of a cat but they can be easier than dogs in some ways. They share your environment but will patrol their own territory without needing to be taken out by you. If you have a good size house and garden combo then a cat might be ideal. Remember though that cats have other very complex needs so make sure you can provide for those too.

Fish.

Fish are very calming, beautiful animals to watch and are very popular with lots of people. A fish tank doesn't need to take up much room, but if you look into fish, always consider how much room they would like, because a tiny bowl can be just as bad as an unwalked dog. Please, if you do look into keeping fish, find out about where they come from. Some will be taken from the wild and this could be very damaging to the place they come from and the animals and plants that live there.

Exercise

I think of this 'E' as energy you need to care for your pet as well as exercise. No matter what dog you get, you have to go out and they need lots of energy devoted to them and to their exercise and mental stimulation needs. I suspect this is their most neglected need, because lots of people are so busy and tired from normal life. If you've been honest enough to admit you found the exercise hard to fit in, then I am very proud of you. You will have avoided a very sad dog. You never know, later on things might change and you might find that you do have the time and energy to get a dog. For now, what might be better?

Cats As we said with place, cats are very different to dogs in lots of ways. They are pretty independent and especially if you let them go out they can take care of lots of their exercise on their own. They still need energy devoted to their needs, and if your cat likes to stay in, you will still need to make time to help them exercise and play. This could be much easier where you live than finding somewhere to exercise a dog properly.

Rabbits, guinea pigs and small furries None of these animals needs to be walked but they will still need you to devote some energy to making sure their environment lets them get enough exercise and stimulation. This is really important for their health and happiness. As we said with cats, though, this might be very easy for you if you had plenty of time at home but not enough time and space to go out to exercise a dog.

Fish Fish need very little besides your time and money, so could be a great alternative to a high-energy pet like a dog. Remember what we said about finding out about where they come from and protecting their original environment.

Time

In your virtual month, especially in the last week, you should have found that your dog needs a good two to three hours of your time every day and sometimes more. This might not sound a lot to many people, but when you actually have to do it day in and day out, it can quickly become difficult to find the time. You probably won't be surprised to hear that lots of non-pet-detective owners don't realise the time needed until it's too late and pretty soon we're back to that neglected and forgotten dog or an abandoned pet.

Time is very precious to lots of people. We live in busy times. Lots of parents work, lots of kids do a million after-school activities and weekends disappear in the blink of an eye. Trying to find a spare few hours every day can be a massive headache for any family, even if you share the work. All pets need some time commitment from you and it's definitely worth considering right now if you found time an issue at all in your virtual month. It's better not to have a pet than to have an unhappy, badly looked-after one.

Time and energy go hand in hand. If you struggled to find the time for a dog, then many pets like rabbits and guinea pigs might be the same. They need time devoted to making sure their hutch or run is exciting and interesting. You need to spend time handling them and feeding and cleaning, so do your research and try a virtual month with rabbits or guinea pigs to make sure you can manage.

Chapter 9

In some ways cats and small furries may need a lot less time than dogs. It will vary depending on the animal, and as always, research will be important. All pets will need some time for cleaning and feeding, but again that will vary depending on the animal and the size of their cage, how they live and how dirty they are!

Fish could well be another good alternative, but as with the energy required, some like marine fish might need more time than others to keep their tank exactly right.

Time is a precious commodity, and so is money...

Spend

The cost of keeping pets is probably the most massively underestimated thing of all when it comes to owners. Stuff like bedding, toys and cages are easy things to work out and think about, but people always forget things like vets' bills, vaccinations and, quite shockingly, the cost of food. Feeding an animal for two to twenty years can make a big hole in your wallet!

The PDSA PAW report in 2015 asked lots and lots of owners how much they thought it would cost to look after a dog, cat or rabbit for the whole of its life. Most people thought it would cost £1000–£5000 for a dog, when, as we said before, depending on the breed, it can be up to a staggering £31,000! Even the lowest average cost is £16,000 for a dog. Most people gave the same answer of £1000–£5000 for a cat, but the average is actually a whopping £17,000. The average rabbit costs £9000 each, but when owners were asked what they thought it would be, nearly all of them said about £1000.

You can see why people are shocked when they actually get the animals! Money is a really big reason pets get given away. As I said, some people are shy when it comes to talking about money, but if you're thinking of getting a pet, it's absolutely vital you find out how much it is likely to cost and make sure your family can afford it.

From these numbers you'll have already guessed that if a dog was too much of a strain moneywise, then a cat might well be too.

Rabbits, guinea pigs and small furries In general, the smaller an animal is, the shorter its lifespan and possibly lower overall cost. For instance, a rabbit can live up to ten years, a guinea pig around five years, hamsters two years and mice up to a year. The smaller the animal, in general the smaller the cage and smaller volumes of food you need, so on average the smaller ones should be cheaper than a dog to keep. Some of the more exotic ones will be very different, though, so do your research.

Fish Fish will be really variable depending on how many and what type you have. They have hugely different needs for things like water temperature, food and care. A couple of coldwater, freshwater fish will definitely be cheaper than a dog, but a state-of-the-art tropical underwater heaven may not!

What if You're Worried You Can't Manage Any Pet?

Above all please believe me when I say that it is better not to get a pet at all than to neglect one. Being a responsible pet owner is all about making the right choice, and sometimes that means not getting one at all. Try not to be too downhearted. Look at all your options and also think about ways things might change with time. When I was very little we had no spare money at all, but as we got older my mum and dad worked hard and trained and got different jobs and as time went by we found we could get a dog. Believe me, I pestered for a long time before that actually happened!

If you have friends who have pets, ask if you can spend time with their animals and help them with the jobs. You never know, they might be a bit bored with it and might love to have a helper. Just being around animals is a brilliant feeling, so you might need to just take small opportunities when they come along.

Talk to your mum and dad about fostering pets. There are so many unwanted pets, that lots of adoption centres often need people to foster animals while they are waiting for a home. This might mean having rabbits, small furries and even cats and dogs if you can manage, but just for a short time and often with help from the charity with the costs. You'll get some animal time but also be doing a really good deed too.

Be a dog walker. Depending on your age, you or you and your parents could volunteer to walk dogs. This could be for an adoption centre or just dogs in your town or village. Lots of people might be struggling to find the time for their own dog and might love to have the offer of someone to walk them more often.

You could also find out about charities like Hearing Dogs for Deaf People. Some of the centres ask people to care for a dog in the evenings and over the weekends while they're being trained. This means if your mum and dad are at work during the day, the dog just comes to you for the times you're all at home. They have lots of different volunteering options on their website, so you might find something that is perfect. A temporary arrangement might be a great compromise for you and your family.

So here we are, almost at the end of your journey into the wonderful world of dogs and being an A-grade owner. All that's left to say is...

Chapter 10

WELL DONE, DETECTIVES!

By the time you get to here, you will have worked hard and learned exactly what it takes to be an excellent pet owner. Let's think about all the amazing things you have done and achieved since page 1:

🐾 You've learnt about how animals can make us happy and what it means to be a responsible pet owner, including the serious stuff about the law!

🐾 You've found out where dogs came from, how wild dogs live, what makes them happy and what keeps them healthy.

🐾 You've found out what food is best for a dog, how much food they need and how to tell if they are too fat or too thin.

🐾 You've learnt that lots of human foods are bad or even poisonous for dogs.

🐾 You've discovered what sort of environment will keep your dogs happy and safe.

🐾 You've learnt that dogs are social creatures like humans. They don't like to be left on their own for long.

🐾 You've found out that it's very important to let animals behave normally. A dog will need to be able to play, run, interact with humans and other dogs in the right situations and get away from people and other animals when he wants to be alone.

🐾 You know how very important it is to socialise and train your dog and that you should never ever buy a puppy if you haven't seen its mother.

🐾 You've learnt that most animals don't like being hugged and kissed like humans do. It's important not to crowd or follow a dog or hug it. Never stroke or touch a dog you don't know if you haven't asked the owner.

🐾 You've learnt about, obesity, vaccinations, fleas and worms, neutering, microchipping and all the things you need to look out for to spot a poorly dog before it gets too bad.

🐾 You've learnt that some body shapes are not natural and can cause lots of problems for dogs. These shapes are best avoided.

🐾 You've done extra research, spoken to vets and nurses, been to pet shops, looked online, done lots of maths and maybe even made your whole family sit down together to discuss this whole pet-owning business.

🐾 Hopefully you've even gone the whole hog and made yourself feel a bit silly wandering round the garden or the village pretending to do stuff with a pretend dog.

THAT is a very impressive list of things and that is why you should feel very proud of yourselves. I am ecstatic that you bought or borrowed this book and read it and I am very proud of you. You may feel like kids are ignored sometimes and you might feel sometimes like no-one really listens to your opinions, but I'm going to let you into a secret: you kids can change the world. Let's face it, grown-ups have messed up pet keeping for hundreds of years. They think they're too busy to do research and lots of them think they know everything already!

Just imagine if you told your mum or dad all the things you'd learned about how to actually care for a dog. I bet they would be astounded. I bet you could teach them some things. They might think it's fine to leave them all day while everyone is out. But now YOU know better. You might not feel like you can change the world, but if all the children in the world learnt what you have and really took it on board, then pet keeping would transform overnight. Old, wrinkly vets like me would smile and put our feet up because our workload would halve in an instant because of all those well cared-for, healthy pets.

I've told you repeatedly that you should never ask yourself what sort of pet you want, but now we're at the end of your journey I think it's time for you to do just that. You see, it's very important that you ask yourself what sort of animal you can care for properly, but you do also need to consider what you're looking for in a pet, because you and your family need to be happy too. You might have discovered that you can perfectly care for a million dogs, but if *you* wanted a pet that didn't leave hair and mud everywhere, then a dog will never make *you* happy! Owning pets is a team game, so make sure you all talk about your options. If a dog isn't right for you, have a look at the other books in the series and keep learning. I think all animals are fascinating to learn about even if you don't end up with one.

If you've decided a dog would make you happy and that you can keep one or more of them happy and healthy, hang onto the book. Unless you've got a brain the size of a planet, you might want to remind yourself of things when you get your new bundles of joy. When you're deciding where to get your dog, please remember adoption centres and the importance of rehoming animals. There are, sadly, always plenty of wonderful animals looking for a loving home.

If a dog now seems like the worst choice in the world, then pass the book on. You could give it to a friend or sell it for some pocket money. If you've got a friend with a dog you don't think is being very well looked after, you could slip the book into their school bag as a nudge in the right direction. If that friend makes a change to improve their dog's life, then you've taken one more step towards changing the world.

At the start of the book we said that living with animals can be wonderful. I hope the books in this series will help to guide you and your family to what will be a fantastic friendship and a time that you will look back on with big smiles and a mountain of happy memories.

All that remains for me to do is to tell you again how brilliant you are and to award you with your detective certificate. Proof that you now know pretty much everything there is to know about the needs of dogs.

WELL DONE!

Be happy!

THIS IS TO CERTIFY THAT

- -

HAS LEARNT PRETTY MUCH **EVERYTHING**
THERE IS TO KNOW ABOUT CARING FOR DOGS
AND BEING AN EXCELLENT PET OWNER!